CHURCH AND COMMUNITY IN SOUTH LONDON
ST SAVIOUR'S, DENMARK PARK 1881-1905

CHURCH AND COMMUNITY IN SOUTH LONDON

ST SAVIOUR'S, DENMARK PARK 1881-1905

RICHARD OLNEY

HISTORY INTO PRINT
56 Alcester Road,
Studley,
Warwickshire,
B80 7LG

www.history-into-print.com

Published by History Into Print 2011

© Richard Olney, 2011

Richard Olney has asserted his rights in accordance with the Copyright, Designs and Patents Act 1988 to be identified as the author of this work.

All rights reserved. No part of this publication may be reproduced, stored in a retrieval system, or transmitted in any form or by any means, electronic, mechanical, photocopying, recording or otherwise, without the prior permission in writing of the publisher and the copyright owners, or as expressly permitted by law, or under terms agreed with the appropriate reprographics rights organization. Enquiries concerning reproduction outside the terms stated here should be sent to the publishers at the UK address printed on this page.

The publisher makes no representation, express or implied, with regard to the accuracy of the information contained in this book and cannot accept any legal responsibility for any errors or omissions that may be made.

A CIP catalogue record for this book is available from the British Library.

ISBN: 978-1-85858-335-8

Typeset in Minion Pro
Printed in Great Britain by
Information Press Ltd.

CONTENTS

Tables vi
Maps vi
Illustrations vii
PREFACE viii
INTRODUCTION xi

PART I: THE SUBURB 1
1. Making a new district 2
2. Small respectabilities 11

PART II: THE CHURCH 21
3. The creation of the parish 22
4. The clergy 34
5. The framework of church life 43
6. Ways and means 54
7. Worshippers and workers 60
8. A friendly community 70

PART III: CONNECTIONS 77
9. 'Imaginary lines': the boundaries of the parish .. 78
10. St Saviour's and the Church in south London 89
11. Our dissenting brethren 93
12. Education 98
13. Poor people 102
14. Life and leisure in south London 108
15. Concluding remarks 113

PRINCIPAL SOURCES 120
INDEX 125

TABLES

I	The Peckham Rye and Denmark Park estates: social composition (heads of households)	20
II	St Saviour's: social composition of communicant families	67
III	St Saviour's: social composition of baptismal families	68
IV	St Saviour's and neighbouring churches: social composition of baptismal families	69
V	St Saviour's: residence of baptismal families	86
VI	St Saviour's and neighbouring churches: residence of baptismal families 1896	87
VII	St Saviour's (baptismal families): gains from and losses to neighbouring parishes	88

MAPS

I	Camberwell, Peckham and Dulwich c1870, showing built-up areas	4
II	The parish and its immediate environs c1890	28
III	St Saviour's and surrounding parishes c1890, showing boundaries	82

ILLUSTRATIONS

1. Danby Street looking east *c*1900	i
2. St Saviour's Church, east front: architect's impression	i
3. St Saviour's Church, interior looking east: architect's impression	ii
4. St Saviour's Church, interior looking east *c*1925	iii
5. Copleston Centre Church (St Saviour's), east front, from Copleston Road 2009	iii
6. Francis Peek (1834-1899)	iv
7. The Revd John Stephenson, first vicar of St Saviour's	iv
8. The Revd Herbert Swithinbank, second vicar	v
9. The Revd John Haslam, third vicar	v
10. The parish of St Saviour's *c*1890	vi
11. The former Vicarage, 24 Grove Hill Road *c*2004	vii
12. The former Institute, 93 Choumert Road *c*1969	vii
13. The former Church House, 50 Copleston Road 2009	viii
14. St Saviour's Cricket Club fixture list 1883	viii

PREFACE

THIS SMALL BOOK is about a lower middle-class London suburb and the parish church that served it. It is not a conventional parish history, and some readers may be disappointed to find comparatively few details of the lives and ministries of the first three incumbents, or of patterns and forms of worship. This is partly because the surviving sources are not very forthcoming in these areas, but mainly because I have chosen to concentrate on the social history of the parish and the role of the church in the local community.

At the risk of introducing too personal a note, it may be relevant to say a word about how I came to write this book. Although not a member of the Copleston Centre Church, as St Saviour's is now known, I do have some personal and family connections with some of the topics discussed in these pages.

None of my late nineteenth-century forebears lived in the immediate neighbourhood of Peckham Rye, but a hundred years ago they would not have felt out of place there. They were all Londoners, and contributed in various ways to the great late nineteenth-century expansion of the Capital. Of my great-grandfathers, one was a main-line engine driver and a small rentier landlord; one was a provision merchant who at one time owned several shops; another was a commercial traveller; and the fourth was a builder and owner of houses. In the next generation my grandfather – my father's father – was a commercial clerk, and his wife was a buyer for a well-known south London department store before their marriage. They were both staunch High Church people, and brought up their family accordingly. Their son became a churchwarden like his father. Of their two daughters, one married a clergyman and the other a clergyman's son. I myself was brought up in outer-suburban Surrey, and at one period in my youth was a server at our parish church.

My wife and I came to live in the parish of St Saviour's in 1976, and I soon realised that there were parallels between the outer suburb of the 1950s and the inner suburb of the 1890s. Once I began to work on the history of the parish other reasons emerged for concentrating on its early years. This was its formative period, when what began as a new church and a new suburb gradually settled into a more established role as part of a wider south London society. The records, moreover, were relatively full for the period 1881-1905, with surviving numbers of the parish magazine a particular boon for the historian.

The Revd Ian Owers (vicar 1977-82) and the Revd Cecil Heatley (vicar 1982-2007) kindly gave me access to parish records and encouraged my work on them. Without their friendship and interest I would not have started on this project, although naturally neither of them can be held responsible for how it has turned out. The Revd Dianna Gwilliams, currently vicar/priest in charge, allowed me to reproduce items remaining, at the time of going to press, in parish custody, and very helpfully explained the significance of parish boundaries in a modern context. I am also grateful to Charles Howard (churchwarden) for making material available.

My research was also greatly helped by frequent visits to Southwark Local History Library, where, like so many others, I benefited from the unstinted advice and guidance of Stephen Humphrey and his colleagues. For access to records and other material I would also like to thank the staff of London Metropolitan Archives, who kindly made available parish records before they had been catalogued; the Revd Frog Orr-Ewing at All Saints, Blenheim Grove, Peckham and Maureen Abbott, the archivist at St John's, Goose Green, East Dulwich for allowing me to consult parish records; the Revd Dr Nicholas Read and Julia Jones at Holy Trinity, New Beckenham for help in connection with the portrait of Francis Peek; Roger Gajadhar, archivist and records manager at the British Land Company, for making available early printed material relating to the firm; Nigel Scales and Brian Saxton of the De Laune Cycling Club for help in connection with the former St Saviour's Institute; and the staffs of The National Archives, the British Library, Lambeth Palace Library and the Church of England Records Centre, the RIBA's British Architectural Library, the Minet

Library (Lambeth), Lewisham Local Studies Centre and Tunbridge Wells Reference and Local Studies Library.

Rod Ambler, John Beasley, Matthew Cragoe, the Revd Roy Dorey and Jim Obelkevich gave much appreciated advice and encouragement. I am also very grateful to Elizabeth Williamson, Christopher Currie, Gillian Draper and other fellow-members of the Localities and Regions seminar at London University's Institute of Historical Research who commented so helpfully on a paper with the same title as this book.

For permission to reproduce photographs and other material I am indebted to Southwark Local History Library (the early photograph of Danby Street), the Vicar and Churchwardens of St Saviour's (items from the parish records), the Vicar and Churchwardens of Holy Trinity, New Beckenham (the portrait of Francis Peek), Bishop CL Green of the Latter Rain Outpouring Revival Ministries (the photograph of the former Church House), the De Laune Cycling Club (the photograph of the former St Saviour's Institute), and Messrs Kinleigh, Folkard and Hayward, Niche Communications and the residents of Hill House, 24 Grove Hill Road (the photograph of the former St Saviour's Vicarage).

In matters photographic I was very fortunate to have the help and advice of Claire Grey, who was most generous with her time, and without whose expertise it would not have been possible to assemble the various illustrations for this volume in a usable form. She holds the copyright of her photographs of the church and the former Church House.

My daughter Marian and my son Thomas gave valuable advice in their respective fields of expertise as the volume was passing through the press. My wife Ruth has been my adviser and consultant throughout, and in the process has probably learnt more than she would ideally have liked about the anatomy of a small London parish in the late nineteenth century.

I am most grateful to History Into Print for publishing this volume, and to Alan Brewin and his colleagues for their expert help and guidance.

Richard Olney
January 2011

INTRODUCTION

THE PAROCHIAL SYSTEM lies near the heart of the Church of England. It provides for the support of its clergy, but it also links organised religion to ideas of locality and community. In the nineteenth century the system was exemplified most clearly in the countryside. Here the ideal parish would have a church at its geographical centre, and no parishioner would need to walk more than a mile or so to its services. In social terms the church would be an integral part of an ordered hierarchy, with the parson near the top and the labouring poor, occupying the free seats in the church, at the bottom. Squire, parson, farmers, tradesmen and labourers would be bound together by reciprocal ties, often deriving from the fact that in one way or another they all drew their livelihoods from the land.

This, however, had always been more of an ideal than an actuality. The parochial system had never been uniformly applied to the English countryside. There were many over-large or oddly shaped parishes, or ones where shifts in settlements had left a church marooned among the fields. In many parishes there was no resident squire, and in many, before the middle of the century, not even a resident parson. Changing patterns of employment could weaken the old rural community, with its clear if narrow horizons. Urban parishes, moreover, had always been rather different, and by the early nineteenth century, with huge growths in the population of London and the major industrial centres, the differences were becoming ever more pronounced.[1]

By the 1870s, when this study begins, the Church had been grappling with the peculiar problems of London for several decades. Whereas in the countryside concerns were often focused on the scattered nature of the population, with a growing number of people living too far from their parish church, in the urban areas the biggest challenge was primarily a numerical one. The Church was being overwhelmed by a tidal wave of humanity. The ideal that the parson should be personally available to all his parishioners, and that all should have seats in church, became unattainable in many parts of London. Even on the more realistic yardstick that places in church should be provided for one in five of the population, the Church was fighting a losing battle throughout the century. A programme of church building would be launched in, say, Bethnal Green, only for the ecclesiastical authorities to find that they needed to direct their efforts to Southwark, Newington or Walworth.[2] In the early 1880s the bishop of London stated that in order to provide church places for twenty per-cent of his flock he would need 132 new churches each seating a thousand people.[3] The bishop of Winchester told the Church Congress at the same period that 'England is now a vast mission field, full of half-heathen'. A survey had shown that 'in our large towns half the population habitually attended no place of worship, and are not effectually reached by our present Church machinery.'[4] And this after decades of fund-raising to build sometimes large and imposing new churches.

Money was a constant preoccupation. A prefabricated iron mission church could be acquired for £1,600, but that was no more than a temporary solution. A permanent mission church would cost more like £5,000. If you were creating a new parish to serve a population of around five thousand, then you would be thinking in terms of a church to hold a thousand, and that would cost eight or nine thousand pounds around 1880. Even then the result would not be particularly lavish or imposing – less imposing, perhaps than some of the grander nonconformist chapels being erected at this period.[5] The distinguished church of St Michael and All Angels, Croydon, completed in 1881 for a parish of just over five thousand people, cost £17,000, and that was without the vestries or the tower.[6]

Money, however, was not the only problem. To set up a new parish was a complicated business. Vested interests, especially those of the incumbents and patrons of existing livings, had to be accommodated. The Ecclesiastical Commissioners had to satisfy themselves that the scheme was workable, and in particular that the new parish priest would have an adequate income. They themselves might be unable to provide an endowment, in which case recourse was commonly had to pew or seat rents, in other words to letting some of the seats in the church to those who could afford to rent them on an annual basis. By 1880 this practice was by no means universally popular, but there was not always an obvious alternative.

But why create new parishes, especially in areas where clear boundaries were hard to draw and local communities hard to define? By 1880 some churchmen were arguing that the continual subdivision of individual parishes had gone far enough. One alternative was to devise schemes for groups of parishes or even whole dioceses, but these would cut across local interests, local loyalties and local patterns of fund-raising for church-building. Another possibility was to divide a large parish not into small parishes but into mission districts, with a team of curates working under the general direction of the incumbent. This indeed was tried, notably at St Mary's, Portsea. But despite experiments of this kind the parochial model remained the norm, as the Church persevered in its ad hoc efforts to reach the 'home heathen'.[7]

* * * * *

South London had its own peculiar mixture of ecclesiastical problems. The diocesan system was weak. The old diocese of Winchester included a swathe of south London, but in 1877 this was transferred to a newly configured diocese of Rochester. This lightened the bishop of Winchester's load, but for many in south London Rochester was not particularly easy of access. The ancient south London parishes of Camberwell, Lambeth and Battersea contained some densely built-up areas, but also straggled several miles southward into what in the mid-nineteenth century were still semi-rural districts. In Camberwell, for instance, the extensive outer suburban area of East Dulwich was formed into the parish of St John the Evangelist, Goose Green in 1865.[8] Here the population, though scattered, was still not very substantial at that date. But the 1870s saw another great wave of house-building. As the *South London Press* observed at the end of the decade, 'new worlds have sprung up at Clapham, Battersea, Wandsworth, Brixton, Peckham, Nunhead, Camberwell, East Dulwich and Norwood.'[9] Of these places four – Peckham, Nunhead, Camberwell and East Dulwich – were in the old parish of Camberwell. In 1871 it already contained several new ecclesiastical districts, or daughter parishes. In the next decade its total population rose by 75,000, requiring, on the usual reckoning, the building of no fewer than fifteen more churches.[10]

The problem was social as well as demographic. South London had never been as fashionable as some districts north of the river,[11] and by 1880 the number of its seriously wealthy inhabitants – those who could contribute substantially to church extension from their own pockets – was shrinking. When they left these suburban gentlemen were not replaced. Their villas were demolished, and their gardens and paddocks built over with streets of much smaller houses, designed for clerks and artisans. As the *South London Press* put it, 'the large army of clerks would seem to have settled upon Camberwell, to have made it their own, and the men of higher degree have migrated to more congenial districts.'[12] The bishop of Rochester claimed at the same date that the rate of 'immigration of the artisan class into our suburbs' had been measured at 35, 000 a year.[13] In 1874 the vicar of St John's, Goose Green explained to the Ecclesiastical Commissioners that a large number of houses had been built in his parish 'which are rented at from £20 to £30 a year, and furnish accommodation for persons of very small means – quite unable to pay pew rents. This class is continually increasing while on the other hand the more wealthy residents have left the place and gone to live farther out of London.'[14] He exaggerated a little, but as the occupant of a poorly endowed living largely dependent on seat rents he was right to be concerned for his livelihood. It was from this parish that, a few years later, the parish of St Saviour's, Denmark Park was to be formed.

* * * * *

As Professor Keith Snell has recently written, the creation and development of new parishes in the nineteenth century raise interesting questions for the historian, questions about 'the on-going vitality of … parishes, the nature of "community" and belonging, issues of administrative efficiency, the separation of ecclesiastical and civil life, and the decline of religious influence.'[15] Such matters have not been ignored over the last thirty or so years: local studies have included those of Stephen Yeo on Reading (1976), Jeffrey Cox on Lambeth (1982), Jeremy Morris on Croydon (1992), Mark Smith (for a somewhat earlier period) on Oldham and Saddleworth (1994) and SJD Green on part of industrial Yorkshire (1996).[16] But these are studies of groups of parishes in an urban context. When examining the 'contours of church action in a locality'[17] there is also a case for looking at an individual new parish, in the hope that it can shed more light both on the formation of parish 'communities' and on their limits and limitations. St Saviour's was not in all respects a typical new parish. It was smaller than most; it had practically no pre-history as a missionary district; and in terms of social composition it was remarkably uniform. Yet this profile may make it more rather than less useful as an object of detailed investigation.

In the following pages Part I describes the new suburb and the people who moved into it. Part II deals with the origins of the church and its parish, and the way in which its institutions developed over their first twenty-five years. Part III considers the church and parish in a wider context, and assesses its role in the developing social and institutional life of south London.

1. KDM Snell, *Parish and Belonging: community, identity and welfare in England and Wales 1700-1950*, Cambridge 2006, pp24-5.

2. In the early 1870s the parish of St Mark's, Walworth was created for an area of only 30 acres, filled with an artisan population of 6,000. (*South London Press* – hereafter *SLP* – 3 Jan 1874.)

3. *The Church Builder* (the organ of the Incorporated Church Building Society), 1882, p13.

4. *Ibid*, 1880, p44.

5. See, for instance, examples illustrated in *The Architect* for 1880-1.

6. *Church Builder*, 1883, pp109-13. The architect was JL Pearson. Towers were often 'phase two' of a church building project, and frequently postponed indefinitely.

7. *Ibid*, 1880-1 *passim*; Snell, *op cit*, p388; Nigel Yates, 'The work of a great parish', in Sarah Quail *et al*, eds, *Consecrated to prayer: a centenary history of St Mary's, Portsea*, Portsea 1989, p28. For the problems that could arise when new parishes or districts were created see for instance Mark Smith, *Religion in Industrial Society: Oldham and Saddleworth 1740-1865*, Oxford 1994, pp32-41.

8. Church Commissioners' records, ECE 7/1/47447 (file for St John's, East Dulwich).

9. *SLP*, 18 Dec 1879.

10. See HJ Dyos, *Victorian Suburb: a study of the growth of Camberwell*, Leicester 1973.

11. As Bishop Thorold of Rochester remarked at the AGM of the Rochester Diocesan Society in 1882 (*SLP*, 17 June 1882). Thorold had a Lincolnshire gentry background, but he had also had years of experience in London parishes.

12. *SLP*, 8 Sept 1888.

13. *SLP*, 19 May 1888.

14. ECE 7/1/47447.

15. Snell, *op cit*, p367.

16. For titles see below, Sources.

17. Morris, *op cit*, p176; and see also Green, *op cit*, p23.

PART I
THE SUBURB

1.
MAKING A NEW DISTRICT

ON 8 NOVEMBER 1871 an old lady, Ann or Anna Ayers, died in a private asylum in Norfolk.[1] It was, one might have thought, an event of no more than local or family significance. Yet it began a chain of events that within ten years had created a new London suburb.

Ann Ayers was the daughter of Bryan McDermott, a Southwark cheesemonger who had done well in business and retired to Peckham. He had invested in land and houses, and by his death in 1814 possessed considerable property in the Peckham Rye neighbourhood and elsewhere. His single largest holding was a group of fields lying between Peckham Rye to the east and Grove Hill, near Camberwell, to the west. Amounting to forty-three acres, it formed a triangle, with a stream running along the base and its apex at the top of Grove Hill. On McDermott's death this property went into Chancery, with the rest of his estate, and there it remained until his daughter's death.[2] This had the effect of preserving it from development, although by the late 1860s some of the lower land had been given over to market gardening, and in 1866-8 a railway line took three acres from the forty-three, cutting a swathe through the higher fields on its way from London Bridge to Sutton. The railway company had to provide two bridges for this short stretch of line, one for the old public way known as Cut-throat (or more genteely Cut-through) Lane that formed the northern boundary of the estate, and one so that the tenant could still reach the top of his holding.

In 1871 the district was still a lightly populated one. To the east, around Rye Lane, there was already a built-up neighbourhood of mixed housing. To the north, on the other side of Cut-throat Lane, the Chadwick trustees were developing Grove Park with good-quality houses, and to the west Grove Hill and Champion Hill were an older suburb, with large villas in substantial grounds. But to the south there was still farm land. (See Map I.) Nevertheless the arrival of the railway presaged further development, and it would not be long before McDermott's fields were filled with streets and houses.

The Court of Chancery moved to divest itself of the estate with surprising alacrity. The forty acres were put up for sale in one lot in April 1872 and purchased by the British Land Company for £12,100, or about £300 an acre. This company had been set up in 1856 as the trading arm of the National Freehold Land Society, itself founded in 1849. The BLC was a property developer, purchasing estates, laying out roads and drains, and dividing the land into building plots that it then sold individually or in small blocks. It worked closely with its parent body, whose object as a building society was to encourage the growth of a class of small owner-occupying householders. At least in its early years, the BLC usually auctioned off its plots as freeholds, with the purchasers being given access to ninety per-cent mortgages through the Society. But it was a commercial business, responsible to its shareholders, and was not bound to follow any one mode of development. Occasionally it re-sold its properties *en bloc*, and in 1873 it began, following the usual London practice, to dispose of some of its lots on building leases.[3]

The BLC could be reasonably satisfied with its bargain. The site was awkwardly shaped, and was damp at the bottom and steep at the top. But the district was pleasant enough, and the estate was within walking distance of a railway station at Peckham Rye – always a selling point. The building trade was in a poor state in 1872, but the Company could afford to bide its time, provided that it did not end up with too many unsold properties on its books. (In fact the upturn was longer in coming than expected, and the BLC would be lucky to get rid of the last remnants of this particular investment before the housing market dipped again in the 1880s.)

Early on the Company had to decide what kind of houses should be built on their newly-acquired property. It had never concentrated wholly on one

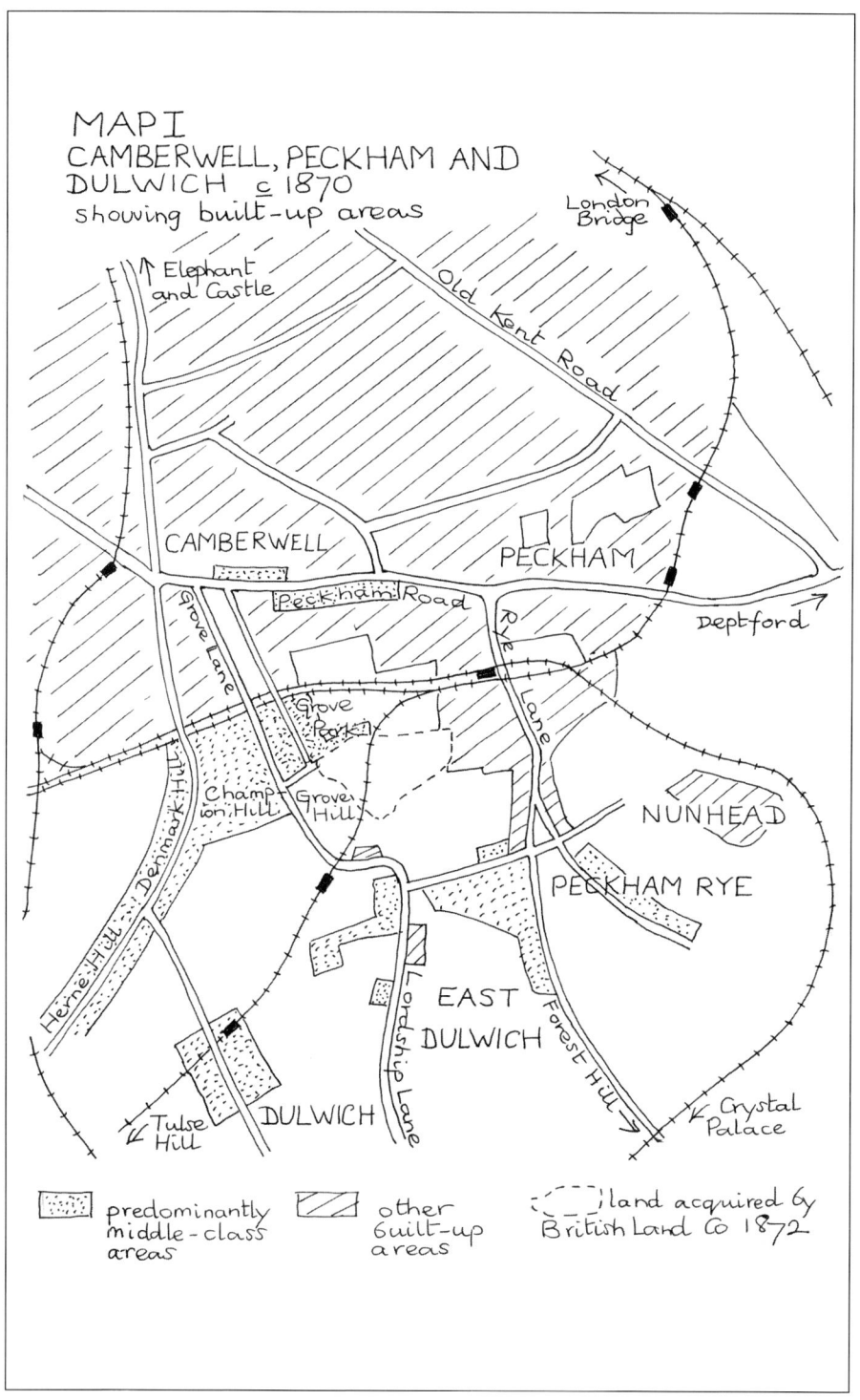

type of housing. Locally one of its earlier developments, Talfourd Road, just off the Peckham High Road, had been built up with mainly middle-class houses in 1857-62. In 1865 it had acquired the large Friern Manor Farm estate in East Dulwich, which slowly filled with a mixture of middle- and lower middle-class dwellings. But the decision was taken that McDermott's fields should be turned into a decidedly lower middle-class suburb. From this every other planning decision followed – the housing density, the road pattern, the building lines, the restrictive covenants and so on. Commercial prudence may have dictated this rather unimaginative way of proceeding, but it did not meet with unanimous approval. The *South London Press* thought that the Company could have done better. 'The locality', it declared in October 1872, 'has a stamp of respectability which demands, in justice, that houses of a reasonable value only should be built.' To judge by the paper's praise a few years later for a development in East Dulwich, 'reasonable' meant houses of an annual value of between thirty and forty pounds, whereas the Company's Peckham Rye development was to concentrate on the £20-27 bracket.[4]

* * * * *

Like the Court of Chancery, the Company moved swiftly. Its surveyors and engineers were soon on the site, and men were put to work even before the Metropolitan Board of Works had given its official blessing to the scheme.[5] Trees were cut down, hedges grubbed up, existing buildings removed, the dyke put under ground, and, in short, every vestige of the old landscape obliterated. Work began with the lower fields, where Bellenden Road was constructed along the line of the dyke. Copleston Road was laid out running north to south just below the railway line, and four further roads, New Choumert Road (from 1881 nos 81-210 Choumert Road), Danby Street, Avondale Road and Soames Street, linked Bellenden with Copleston. Two or three years later the rest of the holding, an area of about eleven acres above the railway line, was similarly staked out. Avondale Road was extended by a bridge over the line, on the site of the former occupation road. Above the line Ivanhoe Road was laid out on a north-south axis, and from it Bromar, Malfort and Grove Hill Roads led to the top of the hill. (See Map II.)

The streets were of decent width, and the houses were to be set back to provide small front gardens; but the plots were to be mostly narrow, and the streets were laid out in a way that made an economical use of the total area. The building plots were meant mainly for houses: there would be some shops, but no unpleasant business would be allowed to spoil the residential nature of the district. On the other hand there were to be no frills of the kind that were a feature of some middle-class suburbs – no impressive central boulevard, no elegant square or open space, no prominent site reserved for a church or superior public house. The children would have to play in the streets, if their parents would let them, and sites for places of worship would have to be sought among the residential or commercial plots.[6]

Another aspect of the lay-out requires comment, and that is the secluded nature of the neighbourhood that was to be created. Bellenden Road was connected with existing streets to the north and east, and at the top of the hill Grove Hill Road provided an exit to Grove Lane and Dog Kennel Hill. But in between the new roads did not break through the old boundaries of the farm, and this created a number of dead-ends. The southern end of Bellenden Road was a cul-de-sac, as were both ends of Copleston and Ivanhoe Roads. Avondale Road, moreover, was the only link for vehicular traffic between the streets above and below the railway line.[7] This situation, which remained unaltered until the early years of the next century, had its effect, not altogether an enlivening one, on the character of the district.

By the spring of 1873 the BLC was ready to start selling the plots below the railway line, an area it marketed as the Peckham Rye estate. Its advertisements drew attention to the nearness of the estate to the railway station of that name, and to the horse-drawn tram service that was now running from Peckham to Camberwell and then up to the Elephant and Castle.[8] The northern end of Bellenden Road was to be a shopping area, and there was also provision for a few shops in Avondale Road, near the junction with Copleston Road. A site for a public house was also suggested on the corner of these two roads, but it was never built, leaving the thirsts of the early residents of the Peckham Rye estate to be quenched in the existing establishments just beyond Bellenden Road. Most of the houses on the estate were to cost a minimum of £250 to build, and this resulted in six- or seven-roomed semi-detached or terraced houses of a very typical contemporary type.[9] Only in Copleston Road were houses of a slightly superior type envisaged: they were to cost £300 to build (a figure revised downward from an earlier and more ambitious figure of £400), and they were to be set back fifteen feet from the road rather than the ten feet specified for the rest of the estate.

Two or three years later the Company was ready to offer the plots on the streets above the railway line. It christened this area the Denmark Park estate, an entirely invented name designed to emphasise its proximity to the middle-class suburbs of Grove Park and Champion Hill as well as the fact that Denmark Hill Station on the South London line was within reasonable walking distance. One might have expected the Company to have aimed for a much better class of house on this part of its development, but it was hampered by the shape of the site. Once the roads had been laid out the space available for individual plots was restricted, and in fact their average size was smaller than on the Peckham Rye estate.[10] A row of shops was planned in Ivanhoe Road, and the Denmark Park estate also acquired a respectable public house, the Ivanhoe Hotel. Otherwise the estate would not be very different from its neighbour below the railway line.

There was one difference, however, and that was in the way in which the Company chose to dispose of the plots. Whereas on the Peckham Rye estate it was more usual for the plots to be sold as freeholds, on the Denmark Park estate two-thirds of the plots were offered on building leases. In both cases the purchasers were generally builders, who then sold the houses once they had completed them, but on the Denmark Park estate the ultimate owners, whether owner-occupiers or rentier landlords, were leaseholders rather than freeholders. To start with the Company retained the freehold of these plots as the ground landlord, but in fact it had no intention of retaining a permanent stake in the suburb, and soon disposed of the ground-rents to a number of private investors.[11] This created an extra layer of ownership for a majority of the houses on the Denmark Park estate, but one that played little part in the preservation of its appearance or amenities.

* * * * *

Though started so briskly, the two estates, as we must now refer to them, took some years to reach completion. Four years after the first plots had been auctioned the Peckham Rye estate still had a gap-toothed appearance. The roads were not made up and the pavements laid until 1878, by which time the early residents had begun to complain of the quagmires through which they had to wade.[12] But the house-building economy began to pick up in the late 1870s, and by the spring of 1881, when the census was taken, most of the plots were built on and the houses occupied. By 1882 most of the streets could be through-numbered for postal purposes, relieving their inhabitants from having to give their addresses as '3 Laurel Villas, Danby Street' or '4 Meadow Terrace, Bellenden Road'.[13]

Just as might have been expected, the Peckham Rye estate was filled with houses of a predominantly lower middle-class type. They were mainly of two storeys, and their recessed front doors, bay windows and small front gardens protected by iron railings all spoke of respectability and social reserve. The average house was neither tall nor wide: the plots were no more than twenty feet in total width, and few houses had basements or attics. Inside there were usually two rooms on the ground floor at the front of the house, flanked by a narrow entrance hall or passage. But behind these rooms would be a 'back addition' containing a kitchen and a scullery. On the first floor there would be two bedrooms in the front of the house, and a third bedroom, perhaps with a box room behind it, in the back addition. The dwelling as a whole was thus larger than might appear from the street, and provided for a good-sized family, the only major drawback of the design being the shortage of natural light. The houses were erected in pairs or short terraces by small builders, who allowed themselves variations in ornamental style if not in basic design, and this added a little variety to the streetscapes.

On the western side of Copleston Road, however, there was a little more variety. A few purchasers acquired double plots and built more substantial houses for their own occupation. On the Denmark Park estate, in Bromar and Grove Hill Roads, there were a number of three-storey houses, that is, houses that could accommodate one living-in domestic servant, but they ascended the hillside in somewhat closely-packed terraces. On both estates the houses were erected to a reasonable standard, although there was a tendency to skimp on the foundations.[14]

No rate book survives for the early years of the estates, but the rateable values for 1900 confirm both the general level of property and the minor variations that could distinguish one street, or even one side of a street, from another. Most of the Peckham Rye estate averaged £21, although the occasional house on a double plot could be rated as high as £29. The eastern side of Copleston Road, however, averaged £24 and the western side £27, with a small number of larger houses at £34 or £35. Denmark Park was not rated much higher than Peckham Rye on average. Ivanhoe, Malfort and the north side of Bromar Road averaged £24, whilst Grove Hill Road and the south side of Bromar averaged £28. There was only one truly middle-class house, rated at £50, on the whole development; and that, strategically placed where Grove Hill Road joined the southern side of Bromar Road, was the Vicarage.[15]

1. Minet Library, Lambeth, deed 12014.

2. For the McDermott estate see The National Archives, Chancery Masters' Exhibits, C104/173 (McDermott *v* Kealy); Lewisham Local History Library, A64/1 (Mayow Adams deeds and papers); Minet Library, deeds 12006-22 (BRA 898); Southwark Local History Library, 1984/256 (abstract of title 1873); Richard Olney, 'Cheese and Chancery: the legacy of Bryan McDermott', *Peckham Society News*, no 103, spring 2006, pp29-32.

3. British Land Company, printed annual reports, accounts and circulars 1857-85; *Register of properties for sale 1 May 1867*; John Weston Smith, *No Stone Unturned: a history of the British Land Company 1856-2006*, 2006. For access to the reports and accounts I am indebted to the Company's Archivist.

4. *SLP*, 26 Oct 1872, 2 Dec 1876.

5. Southwark Local History Library, Camberwell vestry minutes 1872-3; London Metropolitan Archives, MBW 1789, etc (records of the Metropolitan Board of Works).

6. SLHL, roll 60: map of the Peckham Rye estate for sale by auction at the Victoria Tavern 13 Oct 1873.

7. Cut-throat Lane survived only as a short stretch of footpath over the railway (now Copleston Passage): the rest of it disappeared behind back gardens and went out of use.

8. *SLP*, 24 May, 29 Nov 1873.

9. Stephen Muthesius, *The English Terraced House*, New Haven and London 1982, *passim*; Hugh McLeod, *Class and Religion in the late Victorian City*, London 1974, p189n. Similar houses were going up all over south London at the same period, for instance on the Milkwood estate near Herne Hill (*SLP*, 6 June 1874; Herne Hill Society Local History Group, *Milkwood Estate: the story of a Lambeth community*, Local History Publications for the Herne Hill Society 2009, pp11-18).

10. Seventeen to the acre as opposed to fifteen on the Peckham Rye estate.

11. Minet Library, extra-illustrated copy of WH Blanch's *History of Camberwell,* vol 10, p345; HJ Dyos, *Victorian Suburb: a study of the growth of Camberwell*, Leicester 1973, p118. (Dyos's pioneering study is still immensely valuable. His statement (p118) that the Denmark Park estate was sold by the BLC in one lot is however incorrect.)

12. *SLP*, 19 Jan 1878; *Camberwell News,* 19 Jan 1878.

13. London Metropolitan Archives, LCC/AR/BA/05/033.

14. By the end of the century some of the Denmark Park houses were showing signs of subsidence (Sir Walter Besant, *London South of the Thames*, 1912 edn, p285), but they have survived well enough, despite the battering of the Blitz.

15. SLHL, 3687: Camberwell valuation list 1900.

2.
SMALL RESPECTABILITIES

I could lay my finger on lives in the streets around this Church that are indeed greater than the small respectabilities around them.

The Revd Herbert Swithinbank[1]

AT THE TIME of the 1881 census the Peckham Rye and Denmark Park estates were still a very new part of London. Few residents had been settled there for more than five years, and most were very recent arrivals. The census does not tell us how many had come up fresh from the country, but probably a good many had done so. A local historian, writing about the parish of St John's, Goose Green, refers to 'an influx of provincial young couples eager to set up housekeeping.'[2] It is likely that some had met and married elsewhere in London, and had then started in one or two rooms before establishing themselves here.[3] Others had come to the area because of their work, like the colony of Devonian bricklayers in Danby Street.

What the census does reveal is how many of the residents in 1881 had been *born* outside London. For Danby Street, a typical street below the railway line, the proportion was 56% of all adults and as high as 60% of heads of households. As one might expect, more hailed from the southern counties, particularly those bordering south London, than from the north of England. Those brought up in a village or provincial town inevitably came with a set of religious beliefs and cultural assumptions, however they might be modified by later experience. Some may have welcomed the comparative anonymity of a London suburb after the social pressures of a rural community. Others, however, may have sought to recreate in their new surroundings the communal framework that had once been an important part of their lives. More immediately, however, the young couples were busy producing children. In 1881 Danby Street had 173 children under fourteen, or 38% of the population of the road. No wonder the elementary schools of the district were filling up as fast as the School Board for London could build them.

Although the residents of the two estates had come from different parts of London and the country, they were, socially and economically, a fairly homogeneous group (see Table I). Half the households were headed by white-collar workers – commercial clerks, civil servants, warehousemen, salesmen, managers, commercial travellers and others, with a small admixture of journalists and schoolteachers. Within this group there were of course gradations of income and status. The civil servant with a steady income or the managing clerk in a City firm could afford to live in modest comfort. The junior clerk with a young family might well be harder pressed, and have less time or energy for a social life. But even the junior clerk would be distinguishable, in terms of dress and perhaps also social pretensions, from the tradesman; and those in wholesale occupations tended to feel superior to those in the retail trades. Taken as a whole these lower middle-class salary earners were sufficiently strongly represented on the Peckham Rye and Denmark Park estates to set their social tone.

The next largest social group, representing a quarter of heads of households, was composed of craftsmen. Again, they presented a spectrum of income and status, from the small builder with his own business to the young journeyman. The former could be a householder, with an income equal to his lower middle-class neighbours, although he might well lack their security. Locally the building trades were well represented: some of those who settled in the suburb had actually helped to build it.

The remainder, in terms of the occupations of heads of households, formed a miscellaneous group. It included widows, retired people and those with no stated occupations, but the largest element was the shopkeepers, accounting for as many as sixty families on the two estates. Like the craftsmen they were a far from uniform body. A well-to-do tradesman might have one or two assistants, often lodging or boarding with his family. A small corner shop, on the other hand, would depend entirely on family labour. This is a group not easy to separate from the lower middle class on the one side and the artisans on the other. A genteel assistant in a main-street store should perhaps be counted as aspiring lower middle-class, whilst a journeyman baker, although working in, or behind, a shop was really an artisan. On the Peckham Rye and Denmark Park estates, however, the main distinguishing feature of the shopkeepers as a group was that they lived over their shops. This, together with the fact that they had to treat their customers with equal favour, worked against their full integration into the local community.[4]

Also part of this miscellaneous group of household heads were two social classes remarkable for the smallness of their local representation, the middle class and the working or labouring class. The former comprised fewer than twenty individuals, nearly all living in Grove Hill, Bromar and Copleston Roads. They included the vicar, a doctor or two and the odd engineer, surveyor and merchant. Bar the odd carman or bricklayer the working class was conspicuous by its almost total absence.

If one takes all earning adults rather than just heads of households the picture is not greatly different, although artisans formed a slightly higher proportion of the total. In these streets it was normal for the wife not to go out to work, but the children would do so on leaving school, the boys perhaps as office boys and the girls as dressmakers or shop assistants. In one of the less prosperous households in Danby Street the husband was a waiter, the wife ran the house and supervised a small family of lodgers, and of the seven children the eldest boy worked as a page boy (possibly at his father's place of work) and the eldest girl did 'mangling at home'. Such families, however, were not numerous enough to affect the general tone of the suburb.

Servant-keeping is a useful indicator when looking at late Victorian households. A lower middle-class family, where the head earned two hundred pounds a year, could normally afford a living-in maid.[5] In a slightly less well-off family she might be a girl virtually straight from school rather than a more experienced young woman. Those on the rung below that would have no living-in servant, but would make do with a 'doorstep girl' who came in one or more days a week to help with the heavier chores. These girls cannot be identified from the census returns. All one can say is that in 1881 only one quarter of the households on the two estates had a living-in servant. Maids could be found in every street, but were concentrated, unsurprisingly, in Grove Hill, Bromar and Copleston Roads.

Another indicator was the proportion of households in divided occupation. The houses on these estates had been designed for single families, or at least designed on the assumption that they would be so occupied. But from the first the actuality was somewhat different. Just as more artisans came to live in these streets than might have been assumed from the appearance of the neighbourhood, so more people squeezed into the houses than they were ideally meant for. In 1881 145 houses, a quarter of the total, contained lodgers, boarders or whole families of sub-tenants (these latter being counted by the census enumerators as separate households). In Bellenden Road and Danby Street the proportion was as high as a third, but even in the posher streets there were a few such houses. Families of lodgers seem generally to have occupied the upper floor in two-storey houses, with the entrance hall and the domestic offices as shared territory.

* * * * *

The 1901 census shows that the suburb had 'gone down' over the previous twenty years. Grove Hill and Bromar Roads had lost most of their middle-class residents, and craftsmen were more in evidence. Below the railway line the clerks had more or less maintained their numbers relative to the earning population as a whole, but they had shrunk as a proportion of the heads of households. Among the latter working men had made their appearance, some of them connected with road or railway transport. The number of living-in servants declined by two-thirds between 1881 and 1901, and by the latter date they had virtually disappeared from the Peckham Rye estate. Over the same period the houses with boarders, lodgers or families of sub-tenants rose from 26% to 44% of the total. Even Grove Hill Road acquired both a boarding house and a lodging house. In the suburb generally fewer households included children under fourteen, and more families were partially reliant on the earnings of sons or daughters still living at home.

These social changes had been accompanied by demographic ones. By 1901 the immigration of 'provincial young couples' was a less marked feature of the suburb. More 1901 residents had been born in London, and of those a higher proportion had been born locally, in Camberwell or Peckham. One would expect people with such backgrounds to have had more urban attitudes, and more pre-existing local connections, than their predecessors of twenty years before. This change, however, had not been achieved through the natural ageing of a stable population: it was the product of a continuous movement of people in and out of the district. In Danby Street the average length of stay for a family was five years, and for boarders and lodgers much less than that. Of the 101 families in the street in 1881 only 18 were still there ten years later. The next decade was a little more stable: of the families present in 1891, 27 were still there in 1901. This high turn-over had obvious social implications. A modern study has estimated that 'People who expect to move in the next five years are 20-25 per cent less likely to attend church, attend club meetings, volunteer or work on community projects than those who expect to stay put.'[6]

Within this general picture of decline and instability there was one countervailing trend. The clerks actually consolidated their position in Copleston Road, and to a certain extent also in Ivanhoe Road, on the other side of the railway. In both streets a rise in the number of households headed by a clerk was accompanied by a fall in the number headed by a craftsman. In both streets the decline in the number of servants was less steep than elsewhere in the suburb, and Copleston Road also showed a below average increase in the number of boarders and lodgers. This is a phenomenon to which we shall return shortly.

The evidence of the census returns is broadly supported by the social observers who walked these streets for Charles Booth's great *Survey* of London life and labour in the late nineteenth century. At the end of the 1880s they classified Grove Hill and Bromar Roads as middle-class, but downgraded them to only partly middle-class ten years later. The other streets on the two estates were graded as having middle-class elements in 1889, but ten years later this assessment was also revised downwards – to streets inhabited by fairly comfortable families (working-class as well as lower middle-class) on good average earnings. The exception, however, was the west side of Copleston Road, still judged to have a servant-keeping element in 1899.[7]

The reasons for this economic and social subsidence are complex. In the first place, the inhabitants of the two estates were undoubtedly affected by the periods of commercial depression that occurred in the mid-1880s and again in the early 1890s. In particular there was downward pressure on clerical jobs and fewer opportunities for promotion.[8] Rising rents were an additional source of discomfort. As early as 1878 the *South London Press* referred to the effect of hard times on families which had 'enjoyed the seclusion and comfort' of a whole house, but which had been forced to live in fewer rooms 'to evade the abnormal demands for rent and rates compared with their means.'[9] At the end of the century the Booth *Survey* reported that 'the Peckham area is… gradually becoming poorer, chiefly owing to the increased rents which are driving the better class workers further afield to find cheaper house room.'[10]

Whatever the more general economic conditions, however, the Peckham Rye and Denmark Park estates would not have retained their pristine smartness after the first few years. In 1881 the author of a guide to the London suburbs wrote of Brixton that its genteel streets were too new and regular to suit the artist, but that 'this very newness and regularity have charms of their own to the man of business.'[11] But when the charm faded the man of business moved on, probably leaving his house to be taken by a family of more limited means.[12] Rented houses, and especially those in divided occupation, deteriorate over time unless they have good and attentive landlords, and by 1900 our two estates were looking tired and shabby.

Of the two the Denmark Park estate seems to have fared somewhat worse. The writer and poet Richard Church described it as a 'gloomy and featureless quarter' in the early twentieth century.[13] Some of the houses there were now too large for the type of family wishing to occupy them, but tenurial factors were also partly responsible. In 1900 Grove Hill and Bromar Roads had only eighteen owner-occupiers, compared with twenty-two in Avondale Road and as many as thirty-two in Copleston, twenty-three of them on its favoured western side. Moreover a number of the tenanted houses in Grove Hill Road were owned in substantial blocks by absentee landlords. Below the railway line there were many rented houses, but they were a little more likely to be owned by local people[14]

The estates were also affected by changing conditions just beyond their borders. By 1900 the area north and east of Bellenden Road was becoming more urban in character, especially near the railway line and Peckham Rye Station. To the south-west, around East Dulwich Station, the neighbourhood was also declining, 'accompanied by a great rise in rents'.[15] The intrusion of a large workhouse and a poor law infirmary had not helped. Even the wealthy enclaves of Grove Hill, Champion Hill and Denmark Hill had become socially precarious. The big houses were becoming harder to let, and some were being pulled down and replaced by groups of smaller ones. In 1903-5 the fields that lay beyond the southern boundary of the Peckham Rye estate were built over by a council estate of 'cottage flats' (maisonettes) for respectable artisans. These local changes were gradual, and the Peckham Rye and Denmark Park estates themselves were not subjected to any drastic upheaval. No railway goods yard or fever hospital arrived to destroy their residential character.[16] But nevertheless the social slippage of this part of south London as a whole must have contributed to the slow but steady exodus of the wealthier families, an exodus commented on by successive vicars of St Saviour's.

The less well-to-do inhabitants, on the other hand, must have appreciated the improved public transport of the locality. From the start there had been a range of options. In 1880 train travel to central London was still expensive, but over the next two decades the service gradually became better and cheaper. For many, however, road transport was a more important factor in their daily lives. Here the major improvement was the introduction of the electric tram, although this did not take place until just after the end of our period. When the new electric service arrived it benefited not only those who walked north down Bellenden and Victoria Roads to the main road from Peckham to Camberwell but also those who could now walk through the Grove Vale Estate (the cottage flats) and catch a tram in Grove Vale or Dog Kennel Hill. Altogether the Peckham Rye estate in particular was now less secluded from the wider world than it had been to start with. Despite the modern image of the dormitory suburb filled with commuters, there were many on our two estates, particularly in the early years, who worked locally. The population of the suburb, after all, exceeded that of many market towns, and it required services some at least of which could only be provided locally. But by 1905 it is likely that more were commuting. In 1899 Booth's observer noted that 'many leave [from Danby Street] at 5.30 a.m. to catch the early trains and trams.' In 1904 the vicar of St Saviour's wrote of 'a locality like ours which tends to seem dull because so many are away in the City by day, and return weary to rest at night.'[17]

It is sometimes said that neighbourhoods tended to find their own level. Birds of a feather would flock together, and would help to consolidate the social character of a district.[18] On the whole the Peckham Rye and Denmark Park estates do not seem to have behaved in this way. They did not become ever more lower middle-class, but instead became slightly less so over the years. Two points, however, should be made to qualify this. The disappearance of the middle-class families made it easier for those in clerical and related occupations to set the social tone. And there was one street, Copleston Road, where the clerks do seem to have consolidated themselves. It was not coincidental that St Saviour's church was built there in 1880-1.

SMALL RESPECTABILITIES

1. From a sermon on 'My Church', St Saviour's Parish Magazine (henceforward *Magazine*), Apr 1890 (London Metropolitan Archives P73/SAV/J/01/001).

2. WJA Hahn, ed, *A History of the Parish of St John the Evangelist, East Dulwich 1865-1951*, p22.

3. Of nineteen Danby Street families with young children in 1881, in ten cases the dates and places of birth of the children indicate that the families had moved into the street from within the London area as defined by the Registrar-General.

4. Except where indicated, figures given below for the two estates exclude commercial premises.

5. A servant cost about £20 a year in wages and keep, a large item out of a total family income of £150 or less (Muthesius, *op cit*, p44).

6. Robert D Putnam, *Bowling Alone: the collapse and revival of American community*, New York and London 2000, p204.

7. Booth's Poverty Map 1889, revised 1899; *Labour and the Life of the People*, vol II, 1891; *Streets and Population Classified*, 1892; *The Streets of London: the Booth Notebooks, South East*, London 1997; LSE website. Booth's helpers became very good at judging streets or parts of streets from visual clues, although one suspects that even they could underestimate the poverty or near poverty that lurked behind the lace curtains in some lower middle-class districts. In some cases, too, the changes registered in 1899 had probably taken place a few years earlier. See also below, chapter 7, note 2.

8. See Geoffrey Crossick, *The Lower Middle Class in Britain 1870-1914*, London 1977.

9. *SLP*, 6 Apr 1878.

10. *The Streets of London*, p190.

11. [WS Clarke], *The Suburban Homes of London: a residential guide*, London 1881, p56.

12. For a north London example, from a slightly earlier period, see Gillian Tindall, *The Fields Beneath: the history of one London village*, London 1977, pp149-51.

13. Richard Church, *The Golden Sovereign*, 1957 reprint, p111.

14. See the 1900 valuation list.

15. *The Streets of London*, p193.

16. In the 1890s there was talk of driving a road through the Peckham Rye estate to provide a new north-south link, but it came to nothing.

17. Dyos, *Victorian Suburb*, p60; John R Kellett, *The Impact of Railways on Victorian Cities*, 1969, pp367-9; Robert J Harley, *LCC Electric Tramways*, Harrow Weald 2002, p50; *The Streets of London*, p191; *Magazine*, Jan 1904.

18. Crossick, *op cit*, pp33, 49-51; Kellett, *op cit*, p141; McLeod, *Class and Religion*, p4.

TABLE I

THE PECKHAM RYE AND DENMARK PARK ESTATES: SOCIAL COMPOSITION (HEADS OF HOUSEHOLDS)

	%1881	%1901
Middle class	3.5	1.0
Lower middle class	47.0	43.5
Artisan	22.0	22.5
Labouring	2.0	3.0
Other (excluding shopkeepers)	25.5	30.0

Source: census enumerators' returns

PART II
THE CHURCH

3.
THE CREATION OF THE PARISH

THE PECKHAM RYE and Denmark Park estates were the creation of the British Land Company, but that Company had nothing to do with the creation of the parish of St Saviour's and the provision of the church. The story of the church, and hence the parish that went with it, began with the generosity and determination of a single individual who was not a local resident or even, to start with, a local property owner.

Francis Peek (1834-1899) was the son and nephew of tea merchants, and the grandson of a Devon labourer. The most prominent members of the dynasty were his youngest uncle James, who, almost as a sideline, founded the large south London biscuit firm of Peek, Frean and Co, and his cousin Henry, son of James, who became an MP, a baronet and a country landowner in his ancestral county of Devon. Francis himself was born in Liverpool, but as a young man moved to London, where he started his own tea business, Peek, Winch and Co. By the mid-1870s it had a capital of nearly half a million pounds, enabling Peek as its senior partner to draw an income from it of several thousand pounds a year.[1]

At this stage he could have retired from business and led a life of leisure. Instead he continued to apply himself to the tea business, and as a sideline became a property developer, in Lancashire and at Tunbridge Wells.[2] But he also devoted himself increasingly to religious and charitable work, with particular interests in religious education, Poor Law matters and charity reform. He joined the School Board for London as a representative of the City, and set up a fund to give bibles as prizes to Board School pupils. A keen supporter of the Charity Organisation Society, he opposed indiscriminate doles to the poor, and indeed became a little cantankerous on the subject as he grew older, publishing books with titles such as *The Workless, the Thriftless and the Worthless* (1888).

In religious matters he could be described as an Evangelical, but he disliked party labels and had a simple, bible-based faith. Not untypically of prominent Anglican laymen in the London area, he had a nonconformist family background[3], and had no time for ritualism, attacking it in print; but he liked bright and cheerful services, and was fond of a good sermon. He promoted his faith not only through his writing and his charitable work but also through a generous support of church extension in south London.

Although he lacked an immediate local connection with Peckham Rye he did not live very far away. He settled on Sydenham Hill (just in the civil parish of Camberwell), where he lived in some style while continuing to commute to his office in the City.[4] His interest in church building can be traced back to his Liverpool days, when he helped to provide a place of worship for the seaside suburb of Waterloo. At Sydenham he became involved in a working-class district of nearby West Dulwich, home to some of the gardeners, coachmen and others who worked for the 'wealthier families of the neighbourhood'. He provided an iron church, found a minister for it (who was, or later became, a family connection) and headed the subscription for a permanent building, consecrated as Emmanuel Church in 1876.[5]

His next venture was on a bigger scale. He had joined the congregation at St Bartholomew's, Sydenham, where there were good sermons at the Sunday afternoon children's services. This led to an engagement between the curate, Samuel Whitfield Daukes, and Peek's eldest daughter Lily, and when they married Peek had the idea of providing a new church and parish for his son-in-law. The result was Holy Trinity, New Beckenham, which was also a memorial to Peek's parents. He gave not only the church, consecrated in June 1878, but also the vicarage and the schools, at a total cost of over £20,000.

The new district included the Alexandra estate, erected in the late 1860s by the Metropolitan Association for Improving the Dwellings of the Industrious Poor, and with its inhabitants in mind it was decided that over half the seats in the church should be free.[6]

Shortly after this Peek learned that he would have another clerical son-in-law to provide for. His second daughter Annie became engaged to John Joseph Stephenson, a young curate at St John's, Penge. Penge was very near New Beckenham, and it was through Daukes that Stephenson had got to know the Peek family.[7] A Cambridge graduate, and son of a Dorset clergyman, he was a very likeable young man and a good preacher, with a successful mission at Penge to his credit. In pursuing his plans for Stephenson, Peek's first step was probably to consult Anthony Thorold, who had been made bishop of Rochester, with its new presence in south London, in 1877. And it was doubtless Thorold who put him in touch with Thomas Warburton, the beleaguered vicar of St John's, East Dulwich.

Many years later Warburton recalled how Peek called on him with a proposal to build two churches

> ... amongst the teeming multitudes who lived not far from his own beautiful home on Sydenham Hill. ... The writer well remembers the simple unaffected way in which Mr Peek walked into the vicarage of the parish (from which the districts were to be taken) and ... said that he wished to build a church because he saw how much it was required every day he went to town.[8]

This account is a little confused. Were two churches in question or – more likely at this date – only one? Peek's sentiments, however, were not unusual for the period. A London merchant living in Chislehurst, for instance, told the vicar of Rotherhithe that in his daily journey (by train) to London he had 'noted the rapid growth of humble streets topped only by large public houses and Board Schools, and that his heart was moved by the desire to plant a church in this barren wilderness of bricks and mortar which was rapidly swallowing up the country fields.'[9] In Peek's own family his grand cousin Sir Henry shared his anxiety about 'the increasing heathenism of many of the suburbs'.[10]

Warburton's account, with its slight air of condescension, also suggests that there was a degree of awkwardness about the meeting. Peek may have been unaffected, but he was not simple: he was used to saying what he wanted, and to getting it. The vicar, on the other hand, was not a man of business, and his churchmanship, too, was very different from Peek's. Nonetheless he could not afford to reject a generous offer of help. From around five thousand in the mid-1870s the population of his parish was heading for over 23,000 by 1881 unless some of it was reallocated.[11] A new parish, St Peter's, had in fact already been created at Dulwich Common, and in February 1878 a mission church had been opened to serve a rapidly-growing area east of Lordship Lane.[12] But for the Peckham Rye and Denmark Park estates there was as yet no provision, not even an iron mission church. Although the Bellenden Road area was not far from St John's (though not yet directly connected to it by road), the estates as a whole were somewhat inaccessible, and they were unlikely to have any residents who could afford to contribute substantially to the cost of a new place of worship. It therefore seems to have been settled between the two men that these estates should be made into an ecclesiastical district served by Peek's new church.

* * * * *

Having received the bishop's blessing Peek soon got to work – probably in the early months of 1879 – to find somewhere to build the church and parsonage. It did not prove easy. The most prominent corner plots were already taken, either by the School Board or by the nonconformists, and even the house plots were being developed at an ever-quickening pace. Eventually he secured a site on the east side of Copleston Road, by putting together four house plots and bites out of five more. This was just enough to build a good-sized church, but it would leave no room for a churchyard, let alone a parsonage house. For the latter he had to look above the railway line. In September 1879 he acquired a double plot at the top of Bromar Road (it later became 24 Grove Hill Road), adding another half-plot in April 1880 to make a reasonable garden.[13]

To design the church he engaged the Tunbridge Wells architect William Barnsley Hughes (1852-1928), with whom he had been working on projects in that town since 1875. Hughes had adorned Tunbridge Wells with a Methodist chapel (1878) and a rather pretentious hotel, but in 1879 he was still only twenty-seven years old, and had no Anglican church to his credit.[14] For St Saviour's he produced a design in the then fashionable but rather nondescript style sometimes labelled 'Early English'. As described in *The Architect* for 27 March 1880 it was to be 120 feet long and 60 feet wide, and was to consist of 'nave, square chancel, aisles and side chapels with vestries underneath chancel forming basement'. It was a fairly conventional design, with no High Church emphasis on the chancel and a nave large enough to accommodate a thousand worshippers.[15] Working to a mid-price budget of £9,000, the design did not involve much decoration: the materials were white brick with Bath stone dressings and a slate roof. The basement vestry made good use of the sloping site, and, with houses closely built on either side, the windows were large in order to admit as much light as possible.

On 4 December Peek wrote to the Ecclesiastical Commissioners to say that the drawings for the church had just been completed, and to ask whether he should have them sent to the Rochester diocesan architect for his approval. The answer was yes, but the approval was not easily obtained. Ewan Christian was a formidably experienced church architect, and did not think much of the drawings as first submitted. In fact he could not work out how the building could be made to stand up. He criticised the chancel arrangements and the cramped side entrances, and complained about some of the details. '"False ornamental cast iron hinges" should have no place on church doors.' There was much to-ing and fro-ing before even his qualified sanction could be obtained, but meanwhile the building went ahead. Edward Terry, who had premises in Bellenden Road, was given the building contract, and by the end of 1880 the church was complete except for some final masonry work. Even at this late stage there was a hitch. The east end, next to the road, was found to encroach on the building line specified by the British Land Company, and it was necessary to square both the Company and the Metropolitan Board of Works. Finally Peek was able to convey the site and the building to the Commissioners in time for Thorold to consecrate the church on 22 February 1881.[16]

By that date the Stephensons had moved into their new vicarage. It had a drawing room, dining room, study and parish room on the ground floor, five bedrooms and a bathroom on the first floor, and a further three (servants') bedrooms on the second, making it quite the largest and most comfortable house in what was to become the parish.

On 14 February 1881 a patronage deed was drawn up, vesting the right to present the incumbent of the new living in five trustees – Bishop Thorold (in his private capacity), Dr Warburton, Peek, William Winch (Peek's business partner and himself a subscriber to Church causes) and Samuel Daukes.[17] The next task was to settle the boundaries of the parish and embody them in an Order in Council. To keep matters as simple as possible the new district was to be taken out of only one existing parish, St John's. On the north and east, therefore, the boundary was to follow the old boundary of St John's with All Saints' Blenheim Grove and St Giles's Camberwell, from the junction of Bellenden Road with Maxted Road to near the junction of Grove Hill Road with Camberwell Grove (see Map II). From this point the boundary was to run south-eastwards down the hill behind the houses in Grove Hill and Bromar Roads and across the railway line until it reached the southern end of Copleston Road. From there it was to cut across to the end of Oglander Road. Then it was to travel north-eastwards up the middle of Oglander Road and turn left into the middle of Maxted Road before reaching Bellenden Road as described above. All this was carefully set out in an Order approved by the Queen in Council, no less, on 26 August 1881 and subsequently published in the *London Gazette*.

The effect of this was to create a parish that very largely followed the boundaries of the Peckham Rye and Denmark Park estates (see Map II). There were, however, three points of divergence. The line from Copleston to Oglander Road took in a small slice of two neighbouring fields, but their owner, according to Stephenson, had 'steadily refused' to sell them for development, so this was not likely to cause complications in the near future.[18] On the east side of Bellenden Road, between Maxted Road and the Victoria Tavern, there was a small area that belonged to the Peckham Rye

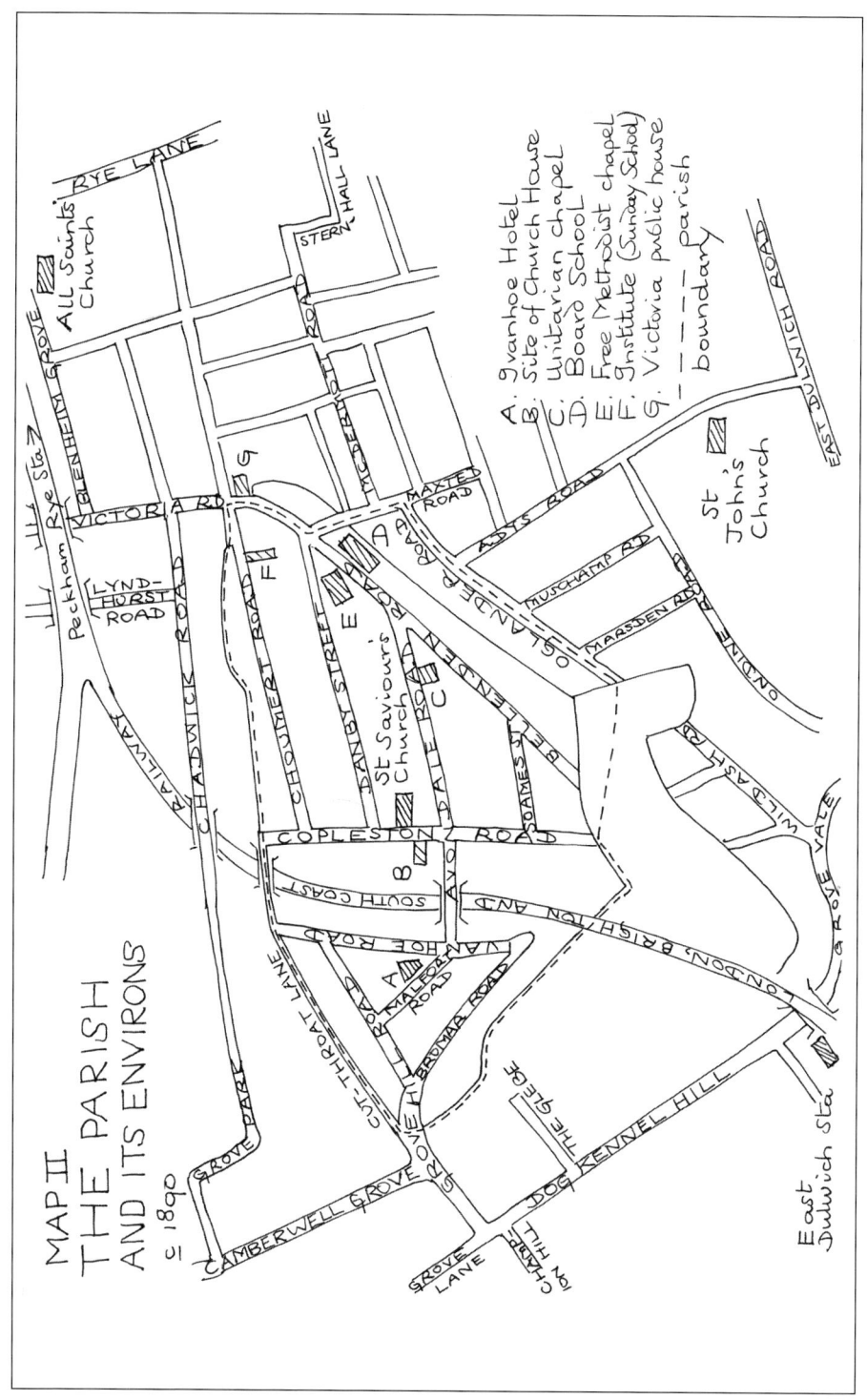

estate but was to remain within the parish of All Saints. Now built up, it contained commercial premises, including Terry's building yard. Finally, and more substantially, the parish *was* to include 2-20 Maxted Road and 2-98 Oglander Road. Nos 52-98 Oglander Road were semi-detached, lower middle-class houses, but nos 2-50 Oglander and 2-20 Maxted were more artisan in character, and also included two or three shops and a dairyman's premises. The effect of this addition to the parish was therefore not only to increase its total population by just over three hundred but also to increase its artisan element. That said, it was not going to make a great deal of difference; but to enlarge the parish any more in this direction would have brought it almost to the doors of St John's. As it was, the Oglander Road houses were nearer to St John's than they were to St Saviour's.

Even with this small enlargement the population of the new parish in 1881 was about 3,650, considerably short of Peek's estimate of five thousand.[19] And of the total a third were children under fourteen. At this date eighty-five or so houses were as yet unfinished or unoccupied, but the figure given in Crockford's *Clerical Directory* for 1884 was still only 4,224. It was much the same in 1901. For a London parish this was small indeed: in 1886 the *average* population of the sixteen districts into which the ancient parish of Camberwell had by then been divided was thirteen thousand.[20]

Peek had wanted to call the new church St Saviour's, Champion Hill. As a dedication St Saviour was unexceptionable. It was favoured by Low Churchmen who disliked dedications to individual saints, and followed Peek's own choice of Emmanuel at West Dulwich and Holy Trinity at New Beckenham. Champion Hill was more problematic, since it referred to an area that lay entirely outside the parish. Champion Hill remained the official title as far as the Ecclesiastical Commissioners were concerned, but Stephenson preferred Denmark Park, and in fact St Saviour's Denmark Park became the accepted local usage. (Strictly speaking the church was on the Peckham Rye estate, but around 1890 it was not unknown for residents of Copleston Road to give their address as Denmark Park.)[21]

One important matter was still outstanding, that of how Stephenson and his successors were to be paid. Peek was not proposing to endow the living: he had spent £8,000 on the church and as much as £4,000 on the vicarage, both site and house having proved 'very expensive' in 'this densely populated district'.[22] Nobody else had come forward with an endowment, and without it the only certain income for the living would be about £50 a year from fees and Easter Offerings. Recourse was therefore had to the usual standby of seat rents.[23] Of the thousand seats in the church it was at first proposed that four hundred would be rented to members of the congregation, presumably at one pound a year. This was modified to three hundred, a more realistic number given the likely social composition of the parish. Of the income of £300 thus generated, however, the vicar would be expected to allocate half to the salary of a curate, thus leaving him a personal income of no more than £200 including fees and offerings. Repeated lobbying of the Ecclesiastical Commissioners, however, resulted in 1883 in their agreeing to provide an endowment of £200 a year. This belated generosity placed the vicar of St Saviour's in a more comfortable position than his neighbours at St John's and All Saints', and was presumably a recognition of Peek's very substantial financial role. In fact they also agreed to allow him £1,500 against the cost of the parsonage.[24]

Despite these concessions one suspects that Peek had not altogether enjoyed his dealings with the bureaucratic and uneffusive Commissioners, and even Bishop Thorold had turned out to be 'much more rigid to deal with than the Archbishop', with whom he had worked in connection with New Beckenham.[25] It is much to his credit, therefore, that he continued handsomely to support the cause of church extension in south London. On Christmas Day 1881 he wrote to Thorold offering to fund a church to hold a thousand people if 'the Christian worshippers of South London and its suburbs' would raise the money for another nine during 1882. The bishop, no doubt by prior arrangement, forwarded the letter to *The Times*, and the Ten Churches Fund was launched.[26] Peek's contribution was another church to benefit the overloaded parish of St John's, Goose Green. The iron church in East Dulwich already referred to was replaced by a church on Friern Road dedicated to St Clement. This time plots were available to build a church, vicarage and Sunday school close together. (The ground landlord was again the British Land Company, but the development of its Friern Manor Farm estate was going less rapidly than it had hoped.) For a design Peek went once more to WB Hughes, who produced a more interesting church than St Saviour's. (Unfortunately it was destroyed by bombing in the Second World War.) Otherwise things did not go as well as they had at St Saviour's. Peek's candidate for the living was rejected by the High Church congregation in favour of their own man, the existing curate.[27] Even this rebuff did not put him off completely. He never again provided a whole church out of his own pocket, but during the 1890s he contributed lesser sums to St Barnabas's, Dulwich, and St Silas's, Nunhead, both of them new churches for parts of the ancient parish of Camberwell.[28]

Peek's achievement in creating St Saviour's was no mean one. It had involved deploying not only his own fortune and family resources but also his experience as a businessman and property developer. He had had to deal with architects, solicitors and ecclesiastical dignitaries. Considering all the interests to be accommodated, and all the authorities to be satisfied, ending with the Privy Council, it is amazing how he was able to bring the work to fruition in such a short time. But one set of people has not yet featured in the story – the people for whom the church was being provided. It was they, and not the bishop or the Ecclesiastical Commissioners, on whom the success of the new parish would ultimately depend. More immediately, however, responsibility lay on the shoulders of a young priest, still in his mid twenties, taking up his first living. A new institution had been created, and it was his task to breathe life into it.

1. Guildhall Library MS 31633, private ledger of Francis Peek, Winch and Co 1855-78.
2. Vera Coomber, 'Architect of Victorian Tunbridge Wells', Royal Tunbridge Wells Civic Society Newsletter, spring 1994, pp11-13, summer 1994, pp1-3. The former Royal Kentish Hotel in Tunbridge Wells still bears the initials FP (for Francis Peek) in ironwork over the entrance.
3. Jeffrey Cox, *The English Churches in a Secular Society: Lambeth 1870-1930*, p113.
4. Liz Johnson, *Dulwich Park: a park for the people for ever*, Lavenham 2005, pp29-33. Not far from Peek lived another tea merchant, Frederick Horniman, who was a leading subscriber to St Peter's, Dulwich Common.
5. *SLP*, 6 Sept 1873, 15 July 1876, 29 July 1882.
6. *SLP*, 29 June 1878.
7. St Saviour's Jubilee booklet 1931, article by Peek's grandson FW Daukes.
8. *Rochester Diocesan Chronicle*, Nov 1899.
9. Revd Eric H Walker, *A Short History of the Parishes of S. Katharine and S. Barnabas Rotherhithe*, 1962; *The Church Builder*, 1882, pp11-14. For the artisan St Helena estate, for which St Katharine's was built, see Donald J Olsen, *The Growth of Victorian London*, pp276-7. The merchant was Richard Foster.
10. Lambeth Palace Library, Tait Papers, vol 285, f75, Peek to Tait 7 Aug 1881. Peek was trying to harness surplus City church endowments to fund suburban church-building.
11. *SLP*, 23 Feb 1878; Church Commissioners' files, ECE/7/112140, ECE/7/1/47447/1. See also above, Introduction.
12. Hahn, *A History of the Parish of St John the Evangelist*, p22. This mission district became the parish of St Clement's (see below).
13. London Metropolitan Archives, Rochester diocesan records, DR/09/49 (St Saviour's parsonage papers 1879-82). The deeds for the site of the church must have been retained by Peek's solicitors, and have not been traced.
14. Coomber, *op cit*.
15. *Architect*, 27 Mar 1880; LMA, P73/SAV/D/01/002 (ground plan in the parish records).
16. ECE/7/1/59883; DR/CP/30 (consecration papers).
17. DR/CP/30.
18. ECE/7/1/59883, Stephenson to Commissioners, [May 1881].
19. *Ibid*, Peek to Commissioners, 3 Feb 1881.
20. *SLP*, 4 Dec 1886.

21. *SLP*, 1 Nov 1890, 18 June 1892.

22. ECE/7/1/59883, Peek to Commissioners, 12 Aug 1881.

23. Of 705 churches and chapels in London *c*1871, only 110 had no rented seats (*SLP*, 10 Feb 1872, quoting Mackeson's *Guide*).

24. ECE/7/1/59883.

25. *Ibid*, Peek to Commissioners, 3 Feb 1881.

26. Mrs Jas A Heaton, *Origins of the Diocese of Southwark 1877-1905*, Southampton 1950, p21. The Fund eventually met its target, although it took longer than planned.

27. *History of the Parish Church of St Clement, East Dulwich*, [1932]. The tone of the booklet is grudging towards Peek, and claims that he had to be leant on by Thorold to spear-head the Ten Churches Fund.

28. *SLP*, 30 July 1892; Jubilee booklet.

4.
THE CLERGY

THE PARISH OF St Saviour's may have been nearly filled with houses by 1881, but pastorally it was a largely untilled field. Clergy from St John's had made a small beginning by holding services in a house in Copleston Road, next door to where the church was to be built. Fifty years later a parishioner remembered that they had been 'attended by a fair number, considering the scarcity of houses in the immediate vicinity and also the condition of the roads, especially in bad weather.'[1] By the time of the church's consecration in February 1881 Stephenson had got a choir together, but it was untrained, and he worried how it would perform on the day, although in the end all seems to have gone off satisfactorily.[2]

Once the church was available for worship he had to construct a programme of services and decide on the tone of his ministry, though he may have done little more than follow his own leanings and put into practice lessons already learnt elsewhere. According to his bishop he held 'all the vital doctrines which are commonly identified with the Evangelical school of thought'. Those who enjoyed ritual would have to continue to attend St John's. On the other hand he determined to eschew the kind of austerity practised at All Saints', Blenheim Grove. In Thorold's words again, he had an 'honest love of Anglican order and worship', and the services at St Saviour's were to be not only accessible but attractive. Luckily his father-in-law was of the same mind: Peek approved of worship in a 'solemn and beautiful setting', and on a visit to the parish in November

1881 praised the earnest preaching, the bright and cheerful services and the good music.³

If this strategy was sound, so were Stephenson's tactics. A good leader, he seems quickly to have assembled a good team of laymen, and to have worked well with them. Not one to stand on his clerical dignity, he declared from the pulpit that he would have liked occasionally to have been able to 'lay aside cassock and surplice, and speak like one of our Dissenting brethren, in every day garb.' In such circumstances it is remarkable how quickly 'traditions' can be invented. Some of the excitement of those early months can still be detected in one of his sermons. 'The marks of the workman's chisel', he said,

> … are fresh about our walls. Only two years ago there was nothing here but a piece of wasteland, with its few tufts of rank grass and its broken rail … But the tie that binds us brothers, though it is new, yet it is strong. Our Church is young, and so are we. She begins her history with us. We take our stand upon the present.⁴

By January 1883 (the date of the first parish magazine to survive) the parish was fully functional, and 167 children had already come to the font for baptism. But Stephenson's health was showing alarming symptoms of breakdown. Periods of absence from the parish failed to restore it, and he died, of tuberculosis, on 1 January 1884.⁵ His wife, aged only twenty-three, followed him to the grave a few months later, leaving the grieving Pecks with two young grandchildren.

The 'widowed parish' held together well, aided by the efforts of two good curates, but it took time to find a successor. Finally, at Easter 1884, Bishop Thorold came to announce that the archbishop of York had recommended a young man from his diocese, Herbert Swithinbank.⁶ An Oxford graduate with a Yorkshire background, Swithinbank was twenty-seven and married. He lacked relevant parochial experience, but was prepared to take on the challenge of St Saviour's after its long interregnum, and was later described as having 'quite exceptional literary and artistic gifts'.⁷ What also became apparent, when he wrote an introductory letter to the Magazine, was that he was a decided high churchman. It was dated 'the Vigil of the Ascension', included a long Latin quotation, and ended by looking ahead to the dawn of a new Catholic era in the history of the English Church.

Once in residence at St Saviour's he made 'a few slight changes' during his first six months, including the appointment of a sacristan and the introduction of a litany desk (an article of furniture that had been prominent in anti-ritualist ructions at St John's only seven years previously). Although he refrained from advertising it in the parish magazine, he may well have worn coloured vestments to celebrate the Eucharist, and have adopted the eastward position (that is, facing the altar rather than the congregation) while doing so, both elements of High Church worship that were becoming more common at this period.[8]

The result, predictably, was a period of congregational unrest. The *South London Press* even referred luridly to 'scandal after scandal'. At the Easter vestry of 1885 some of the vicar's supporters were excluded on the grounds of non-residence in the parish, and the following Easter both churchwardens were objected to, though unsuccessfully, on that score. In 1886 the vicar's warden and the people's warden fell out over the accounts. And in the summer of 1885 there had been a row over the Sunday school: the vicar and the Sunday school superintendent were accused of excluding children from the annual treat on grounds of 'respectability', whereas they claimed it was merely a punishment for poor attendance during the year.[9] These controversies suggest some local and social tensions, as well as a new incumbent asserting himself after a period when the parish had run itself.[10] But dissatisfaction with Swithinbank's liturgical changes, though apparently not voiced specifically, must also have played their part. Having, however, gone thus far he called a truce. Peace broke out at the 1887 vestry, the anti-ritualists seemingly appeased by the unopposed election of a comparatively low churchman, Edwin Gauntlett, as people's warden.

The late 1880s, the period while the truce lasted, were among the most successful in the church's early years. Communicant numbers rose from 310 at Easter 1884 to 522 at Easter 1890.[11] The music thrived under an able organist. The Sunday school grew unstoppably until it had around five hundred children, and the social life of the parish modestly blossomed. In 1891, however, Swithinbank made further changes, introducing the carrying of the Cross in procession, the mixed chalice, the lighting of the altar candles, the singing of the Agnus Dei and the separation of the eleven o'clock Mattins on Sunday morning from the following celebration of Holy Communion (the noisy departure of the Mattins people at the start of the next service having long been offensive to him). The mixed chalice and the lighted candles had featured in the (largely favourable) judgment of the archbishop of Canterbury in the case of Bishop King in November 1890, a case that Swithinbank had been following closely. And it is likely that he was further encouraged by two Oxford friends when they came to conduct a mission in the parish early in 1891.[12]

'Several old friends withdrew' as a consequence, and the number of Easter communicants fell to 495 in 1891 and 411 in 1892. Among the disgruntled was Edwin Gauntlett, who considered Swithinbank unsound on the Real Presence. Early in 1892 he wrote to Mr Spurgeon, the great Baptist leader, to seek clarification: he remembered having heard him preach on the subject in 1854.[13] It is interesting to note, however, that there was no mass walk-out. In matters of liturgy even committed Evangelicals could by this date be fairly relaxed.[14] Only a few knowledgeable churchmen such as Gauntlett appreciated the important doctrinal differences that underlay these somewhat arcane liturgical disputes.

By early 1892 the vicar could claim that the grumbles were subsiding, and that there was 'less of that uneasy suspicion which used to make us all so uncomfortable': even the 'dear old people who "don't hold with such goings on"' were making efforts to 'suppress their private feelings'.[15] Probably his efforts over the preceding few years to educate his flock in doctrinal matters and to inculcate habits of reverence and personal devotion had helped to prevent a major disruption. But his later years at St Saviour's were not as successful as his earlier ones.

The neighbourhood was changing, times were hard for many of his parishioners, and fund-raising became more difficult. His own income declined, and, as with so many parish priests, money worries and health worries went hand in hand. He had two spells of illness, one in the winter of 1891-2 and another in the winter of 1896-7. By 1897 he was on the look-out for another post, and in 1899 he found one. He went to a less demanding parish near Richmond (Surrey), enabling him to pursue his educational interests as a diocesan inspector of schools.

He was followed by John Haslam, a highly-experienced middle-aged priest who since 1891 had been vicar of the populous parish of Gravesend. He had a reputation as a preacher and lecturer, and since 1886 had been a Rochester diocesan missioner. He was recommended to Peek by a former colleague of Haslam's father, a well-known Cornish revivalist. Peek was near the end of his life, and for some years had had little to do with St Saviour's, but he had not been happy with the way things had gone under Swithinbank, and was glad of the opportunity to present a more congenial successor.[16] It is less obvious why Haslam should want to move to such a comparatively unimportant parish, but it is likely that Bishop Talbot wanted him to concentrate on his mission work, and thought that St Saviour's would make a more central, and less demanding, base in the diocese than Gravesend.

Haslam began well by writing a conciliatory letter to the outgoing Swithinbank, stressing that he was coming to take up the work at St Saviour's in 'no mean or prejudiced spirit'. A cultured man and an amateur artist, he believed, like his two predecessors, in the beauty of holiness: he 'retained most of the outward accompaniments of Catholic ritual and worship', and made only a few changes in the services.[17] He concentrated instead on reviving the social side of the parish, which had never featured prominently in Swithinbank's scheme of things and which had declined markedly in his latter years. His major achievement was to build a parish hall opposite the church in 1902.

Unfortunately his ministry did not progress as he or Bishop Talbot had hoped. His engagements in the diocese at large were heavy, but the parish also proved unexpectedly demanding. He tried to run it with one curate, although it really needed two, and when he lost even that help he soldiered on alone. At this point the story becomes ominously familiar. His health deteriorated, and by 1904 he appeared to be in the throes of a major breakdown. Eventually a brain tumour was diagnosed, but too late to save his life. He died in Switzerland, where he had been sent for treatment, in August 1904.[18]

By that date Peek had been dead for nearly five years, but had he still been alive he would have been very happy with Haslam's successor, despite the fact that the choice fell on a moderate high churchman. Francis Whitfield

Daukes was the son of SW Daukes and hence Peek's grandson.[19] He came from a four-year curacy at All Saints', South Lambeth, and had no difficulty in seeing what needed to be done at St Saviour's. He set a more overtly spiritual tone than Haslam, and sought to put the church and its worship back at the centre of parish life. But he also attended to aspects of the parochial machinery, such as the visiting system, that had fallen into disrepair. In all this he displayed ability in practical and financial matters, and a sensible determination not to run himself into the ground. After leaving the parish in 1914 he had a successful career in the Church, ending as suffragan bishop of Plymouth in 1934.

* * * * *

Stephenson had concluded early in his ministry that St Saviour's was a two-curate parish, despite its relatively small size, and a few months after his own arrival Swithinbank came to the same conclusion.[20] Curates were needed to help maintain a full programme of services, assist with bible and confirmation classes, keep an eye on any mission church in the parish, and attend, and often chair, the meetings and events that could otherwise fill every evening of the vicar's week. With luck there would be a particularly young and energetic curate ready to throw himself into that vital aspect of parish life, youth work.

After a rocky start Stephenson was lucky enough to obtain two good assistant priests, J Sinclair Carolin (1882-5) and E Herbert Jones (1883-4). They held the fort when Stephenson was ill and absent from the parish, and Carolin stayed on to ease the transition to the Swithinbank regime.[21] Swithinbank was also comparatively fortunate. WH Wilkin helped to foster the parish's musical life, while Alan Gordon Smith encouraged the cricket club and the literary society.[22] It is no coincidence that their presence coincided with a good period for the parish in general. From the early 1890s, however, there were increasing problems in finding and retaining suitable curates. In fact the curate problem was rather like the servant problem: both were a result of a shift in the pattern of supply and demand. Swithinbank had to come down from two curates to one, and on two occasions was left for a time with none at all.

Haslam was an experienced employer of curates, and not short of contacts around the diocese, but he too ran into difficulties. With greater frankness than his predecessors he discussed them in the parish magazine.[23] He brought with him from Gravesend an acolyte called Horace Sturt, who did excellent work in starting or reviving parish activities but then, after only a few months, went off to a teaching post at Bexhill. From then on it was downhill all the way. A possible replacement went elsewhere because he could not find a suitable house in the parish. Next came EH Clements, who arrived 'somewhat overdone' from an exacting west London parish. He found lodgings with a family in Danby Street but after a short time became terminally ill. His successor, HR Cuffe, appears not to have been satisfactory, and was let go in 1903, leaving Haslam altogether curateless. The problem was partly the pay: the standard salary was £150 a year, 'a very small income for a man well educated and expected to hold a certain position'. Haslam also held that older men with families were generally unsuitable for the work. Younger men, on the other hand, tended to choose parishes where they could get a wider range of experience than was available at St Saviour's.[24]

1. *Jubilee booklet*, 1931.

2. LMA, DR/CP/30 (consecration papers). The ceremony involved the presentation of the deed of conveyance of the church to the bishop, who then laid it on the altar – a nice conjunction of the material and the spiritual.

3. *Sermons by the late Rev JJ Stephenson, Vicar of St Saviour's, Denmark Park, with an introductory preface by the Lord Bishop of Rochester*, 1884; *SLP*, 15 July 1876, 12 Nov 1881.

4. *Sermons,* pp81, 205.

5. *SLP*, 10 Sept 1904. At the time of his death its cause was not mentioned.

6. Records in parish custody, *Magazine*, May 1884.

7. *Jubilee booklet*, recollections of FW Daukes.

8. *Magazine*, Dec 1884. By 1890 there were a sacristan and two sub-sacristans. We are told that 'the S. Saviour's sequence of liturgical colours accords with the antient use of Exeter', and in February 1890 the sacristan read a paper to the Church Workers' Society on liturgical colours. See also Nigel Yates, *Anglican Ritualism in Victorian Britain 1830-1910*, Oxford 1999, esp pp277-9.

9. LMA, St Saviour's parish records, P73/SAV/G/01/001, vestry book 1881-1913; *SLP*, 25 July and 1 Aug 1885, 1 and 15 May 1886.

10. The absence of a minister could have the effect of *stimulating* congregational activity. (Stephen Yeo, *Religion and Voluntary Organisations in Crisis* [a study of Reading 1890-1914], London 1976, p156.)

11. P73/SAV/A/04/001, roll of communicants 1888-1900, with summaries of Easter communicant figures from 1881.

12. *Magazine*, July 1891, Sept 1892. At St Clement's HE Jennings, a high churchman and leading light of the English Church Union, introduced lighted candles on the altar following the King judgment (*History of St Clement's*, p35).

13. *Magazine*, Feb 1892.

14. DW Bebbington, *Evangelicalism in Modern Britain: a history from the 1730s to the 1980s*, London 1989, pp147-8.

15. *Magazine*, Jan 1892.

16. There had been family tragedy, too, at Holy Trinity, New Beckenham, where Peek had continued to serve as a churchwarden. His daughter Lily died in 1889, and her husband Samuel Daukes in 1893.

17. *SLP*, 13 May 1899; *Jubilee booklet*.

18. *Magazine*, Sept 1904; *SLP*, 27 Aug and 10 Sept 1904.

19. One of Daukes's first duties at St Saviour's was to baptise Stephenson's granddaughter. Old Mrs Peek was present, on her first visit to the parish for many years (*SLP*, 11 Feb 1905).

20. Records in parish custody, *Magazine*, Jan 1883, Dec 1884.

21. He later became vicar of St Matthew's, Denmark Hill.

22. *SLP*, 31 Mar 1888, 26 Oct 1889.

23. A propos of the servant problem, Stephenson was able to keep the three servants for whom the Vicarage had been designed. Haslam kept two. Swithinbank, who had no private means, kept only one, although there may have been a daily governess, and he was able to send his son to Eton on a scholarship.

24. *Magazine*, Jan, July and Oct 1900; Jan, Oct and Dec 1901; Feb and Oct 1903. For financial aspects of the curate question see also below, chapter 6.

5.
THE FRAMEWORK OF CHURCH LIFE

ONE SOUTH LONDON incumbent, soon after taking up a living in 1870, stated in no uncertain terms that 'he had begun as he meant to go on; and that with every change of incumbent there must necessarily be a change in the congregation.'[1] Occasionally the change was seismic. When, a few years later, Bishop Thorold (acting as patron rather than as diocesan) put in a new Low Church vicar at St Paul's, Lorrimore Square, virtually the entire congregation voted with its feet.[2] But this was unusual even at that date, and in the following twenty years the disputes seem gradually to have become less heated. At St Saviour's changes in the congregation can be detected in the mid-1880s, the early 1890s and to a lesser extent following Haslam's arrival, but what are more striking are the continuities. The practices of the church and the character of the parish developed in certain ways almost despite the views and efforts of successive incumbents.[3]

A good example is provided by the internal appearance and furniture of the church. Under Stephenson a good start was made in beautifying an initially bare and unwelcoming building. During Swithinbank's time it acquired clergy stalls (1886), a new organ (1887), an east window to commemorate the founder (1890), and a new altar presented by a group of male communicants (1893). In 1896-7 the heating and ventilation, a weakness of the original design, was overhauled. Haslam designed an oak screen for the vestry, carved by a talented parishioner, and panels in the sanctuary in the style of Fra Angelico which he painted himself. The Daukes regime saw a new chancel screen, choir stalls and organ case.

The pattern of Sunday services established by Stephenson was not greatly modified thereafter. An early Communion at eight would be followed by Mattins at eleven, and then by another celebration for those unable to attend the early Communion. Evensong would be at seven. In 1883 as many as eight hundred would attend a full Communion service. By Haslam's day numbers had fallen, but not to a level that would cause any anxiety today. According to the *Daily News* census of 1902/3 there was a total of 566 attendances on the chosen Sunday, 258 in the morning and 308 in the evening.[4]

Music was a prominent part of worship at St Saviour's. Stephenson managed to produce a surpliced choir for the dedication of the church in February 1881, and it was carefully maintained thereafter. The choir led the congregation in hymn-singing, but also enhanced the major services in other ways. At Christmas 1883 a Te Deum and an anthem were introduced into the eleven o'clock Eucharist for the first time. Equally important was the organ. A new one was acquired in 1887, and ten years later it was overhauled and enlarged – a higher priority, it would appear, than the yet-to-be-built church hall. The organist was crucial to a flourishing musical tradition, and St Saviour's appears to have had at least two good ones in its first three decades. They mounted big performances during Passiontide, with choral reinforcements and a local amateur orchestra. *Messiah* was an ever-popular standby, but the parish would occasionally have a chance to hear Rossini's *Stabat Mater*, part of Gounod's *Redemption*, or a new work such as Dr J Varley Roberts's *The Passion*, given during Lent 1902.

Great emphasis was also placed on floral decoration, especially at the principal festivals. Flowers brightened the church in the early years, when it was under-furnished, and they had the advantage for Evangelicals of being liturgically uncontroversial. The vicar's wife was the leading flower-lady: when the Stephensons were absent from the parish at Christmas 1882 for the sake of the vicar's health Mrs Stephenson sent roses for the altar from the south of France. During the Swithinbank era flowers contributed to the rich effect aimed at by the vicar, with particular emphasis on the sanctuary.

Weekday services were another matter. From the beginning the aim was to have a daily Mattins and at least one weekday Communion, but attendances were negligible, sometimes not even a quorum of two plus the celebrant. In September 1883 one of the curates recognised that 'the men are mostly engaged in their daily occupations beyond reach of their own parish church', but appealed to the women to attend. Swithinbank made a similar appeal in April 1890.

> Cooped up in narrow surroundings [he wrote of the womenfolk], with common coarse housework by day, they have little in the home to give a lift to heart or mind. But they must know the bliss of the quiet morning hour in this House of God. They know the lift and widening of the soul that come in these fresh moments while most of the world around us is still in bed.

Swithinbank himself was an enthusiastic early riser: he once experimented with a first Easter Day Communion at five-thirty. But many housewives had their hands full in the mornings, making breakfast for their husbands and children and getting them off to work and school. This left little time for donning church clothes for a morning service before returning to their 'coarse housework'. Later Haslam had to admit that 'in a parish like St Saviour's it is very difficult to select convenient times for special services', and that during the week 'most of our people are away in the City and at business all day'. But there were still many who could attend these weekday services, – 'and for their sake I do wish they would'.

St Saviour's quickly established a pattern of major festivals to punctuate the Christian year. Easter was always the climax, with as big a build-up during Holy Week as the clergy could manage and numerous services on the Day itself. Christmas was important, but so was Hospital Sunday (the first Sunday after Trinity) and the Harvest Festival. Swithinbank, however, was less keen on the last-named than Stephenson, and he did away altogether with the watch night service on New Year's Eve, a popular tradition in many south London parishes.[5] Stephenson celebrated the anniversary of the church's dedication each February, but Swithinbank moved it to All Saint's Day.

Missions, in the sense of a programme of special services reaching out to the uncommitted, hardly featured in the life of St Saviour's. Stephenson's ministry was too short, and Haslam was too busy elsewhere in the diocese. Swithinbank did hold one mission, led by two of his Oxford friends, in 1891. On Good Friday 1895 the Cross was carried in procession around the parish, 'a work which left a deep impress at any rate on the workers', and in the summer of 1896 open air services were held on a still unbuilt-on patch of ground opposite the vicarage; but there is no evidence that these events brought in new people.

Like most London churches, however, St Saviour's undertook mission work in the sense that it tried to cater for a poorer segment of its population that was 'unable on account of home engagements or other causes to attend the Church'.[6] Unusually it had no area that could be described as distinctly working-class, let alone really poor, but there was an artisan element at the bottom end of the parish that was lacking farther up the hill. In May 1882 Peek gave the parish a building at 93 Choumert Road, near the junction with Bellenden Road.[7] Known as the Institute, its primary purpose was to house the Sunday school, but it also served as a parish room and a mission room. As early as January 1883 it was hoped that the children's service held in connection with the morning Sunday school might develop into a short mission service.

Regular Sunday evening mission services, however, seem not to have been started until October 1894, and then the initiative came not from the clergy but from an enthusiastic band of lay readers.[8] By the spring of 1898 they were attracting a congregation of a hundred, but the collection averaged only six shillings, or less than a penny per person, indicating the comparative poverty of those who attended. Later that year, however, Swithinbank reined in this activity, transferring the services to the church and absorbing *Mission Notes*, a small publication emanating from the Institute, into the parish magazine. In January 1903 Haslam revived the mission services at the Institute, but they were placed firmly under the 'special management' of the curate.

* * * * *

Just as infants baptised at St Saviour's might have no further connection with the church, so Sunday school children might not mature into regular churchgoers.[9] Nevertheless the Sunday school managed by St Saviour's was not only very popular locally but also absorbed a significant proportion of the parish's resources. By the end of 1881 the school already had three hundred children on its books, with an average attendance of two hundred. This was about all the Institute could comfortably hold, but the numbers continued to rise, and in 1885 the school was divided, with the younger scholars being taught in hired rooms at the Bellenden Road Board school. During the 1890s, under an able superintendent (who was also a lay reader), there were between 450 and 500 children in total and an army of forty to fifty teachers. In terms of organisation it was held to be a model of its kind.[10] For slightly older children, or for those who for one reason or another did not attend the Sunday school, there were bible classes. One of these, specifically for choir boys, was held in the choir vestry; another was for servant girls. Then there was the Vicar's Half-Hour on a Sunday afternoon and, another of the clergy's direct responsibilities, the confirmation classes.

Swithinbank worked hard to attract confirmation candidates, and by the early 1890s they averaged a hundred, more than might be expected from such a small parish. But he still worried about the 'grave leakage' that existed between Sunday school and adult church membership. In April 1892 he described in the Magazine an encounter with one mother who, on being challenged to produce her son for confirmation, told the vicar that '"His Pa can do nothing with him now", which is really an admission that "his Pa" ought never to have married whom he did.' In Haslam's time the number of confirmations fell as low as 21 in 1902, but in 1905 Daukes managed to get it back up to 54 (42 girls and 12 boys).[11]

It was the lady visitors who passed on to the vicar the names of children of age to be confirmed.[12] Under the visiting system, a well-tried one in south London by the 1880s, each visitor, normally a middle-class matron, would be allocated a street or part thereof, and as well as identifying such candidates they delivered the Magazine, reported cases deserving charitable help, and administered comfort or advice where appropriate. Under

Swithinbank the visitors seem to have met monthly at the Vicarage under Mrs Swithinbank's aegis, but under Haslam the system appears to have broken down, thus adding to the vicar's already heavy workload.[13] Once confirmed the new Church member would be urged to become a regular communicant. With this object Stephenson set up a Guild of St Saviour's in 1881, and later Swithinbank elaborated it with various 'Wards'. He saw it as providing 'devotional and practical support for God's work at St Saviour's, and mutual help towards holiness of life'. By the late 1890s, however, it had become inward-looking and 'cliquey', and Haslam was happy to let it expire.[14]

* * * * *

Successful institutions have a tendency to throw out subsidiary institutions, and so it was at St Saviour's, where a number of satellite bodies soon developed their own machinery of officers, committees, accounts and fund-raising activities. Just as the Guild helped to consolidate the core body of communicants, so the Church Workers' Society, founded in 1883, fostered *esprit de corps* among the choirmen, servers and other key workers. Regarded by Swithinbank as 'the best means we have of "bringing people together"', it was still in existence in 1905, and was in fact one of the very few parochial organisations that did not have to be resuscitated from time to time. Much more complex was the plethora of bodies that grew up around the Sunday school. The children's services became ever more elaborate, with their own choir and harmonium. Weekday activities for the children included the Guild of the Love of Jesus, begun as a sewing class for girls in 1882.[15] It disappears from view around 1892, but the Children's League, possibly a successor, was still active in 1905. Most important of all was the Sunday school treat, an annual outing, normally by train, to the countryside or the sea. So prominent a feature was it of the parochial calendar that it can be regarded as an institution in itself: attempts to curb it by Swithinbank were firmly resisted.[16]

When it came to the social and recreational side of church life the pattern was more fragmentary. For the younger and fitter members of the congregation there were various sporting clubs, and for the less energetic there were musical, dramatic or literary societies, but they mostly had rather

1. *Danby Street looking east c1900.* Southwark Local History Library collection PC 1471. By kind permission of the Library.

2. *St Saviour's Church, ~~east~~ front: architect's impression.* From the *Architect,* 27 March 1880. From a copy in the British Architectural Library, RIBA. west

3. *St Saviour's Church, interior looking east: architect's impression.* From the *Architect*, 27 March 1880.

4. *St Saviour's Church, interior looking east c1925.* From the parish records. By courtesy of the Vicar and Churchwardens.

5. *Copleston Centre Church (St Saviour's), ~~east~~ front, from Copleston Road 2009.* Copyright Claire Grey.

west

6. *Francis Peek (1834-1899).* From a portrait in the possession of Holy Trinity Church, New Beckenham. By courtesy of the Vicar and Churchwardens.

7. *The Revd John Stephenson, first vicar of St Saviour's.* From the church's Jubilee booklet 1931.

8. *The Revd Herbert Swithinbank, second vicar.* From the Jubilee booklet.

9. *The Revd John Haslam, third vicar.* From the Jubilee booklet.

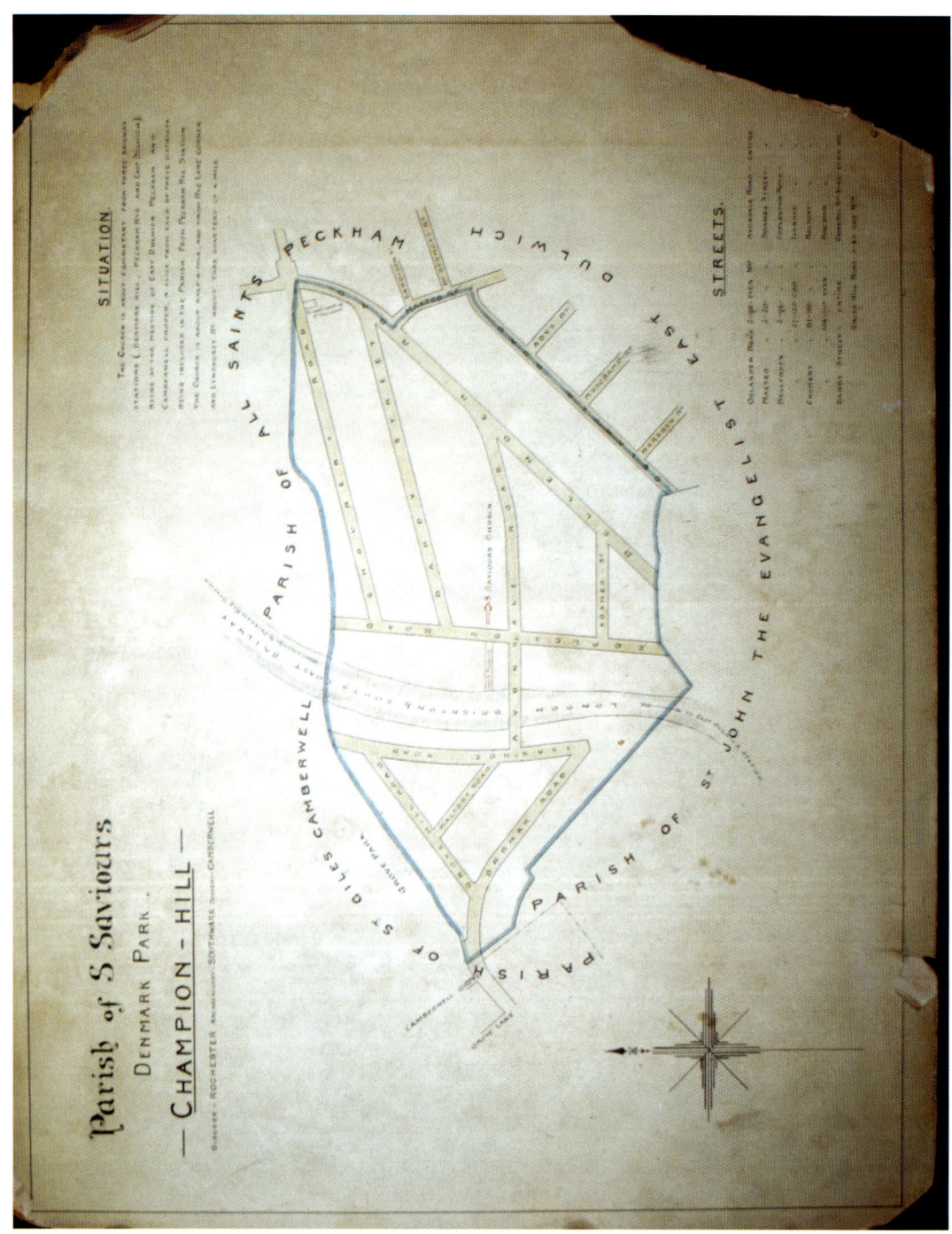

10. *The parish of St Saviour's c1890.* From the parish records.
By courtesy of the Vicar and Churchwardens.

11. *The former Vicarage, 24 Grove Hill Road c2004.* Author's collection. Reproduced by courtesy of Messrs Kinleigh, Folkard and Hayward, Messrs *Niche,* and the management company, Hill House, Grove Hill Road.

12. *The former Institute, 93 Choumert Road c1969.* From the records of the De Laune Cycling Club. By courtesy of the Club. The photograph shows the conversion to a club headquarters already in progress.

13. *The former Church House, 50 Copleston Road 2009.* By courtesy of the Latter-Rain Outpouring Ministries and Bishop CL Green. Copyright Claire Grey.

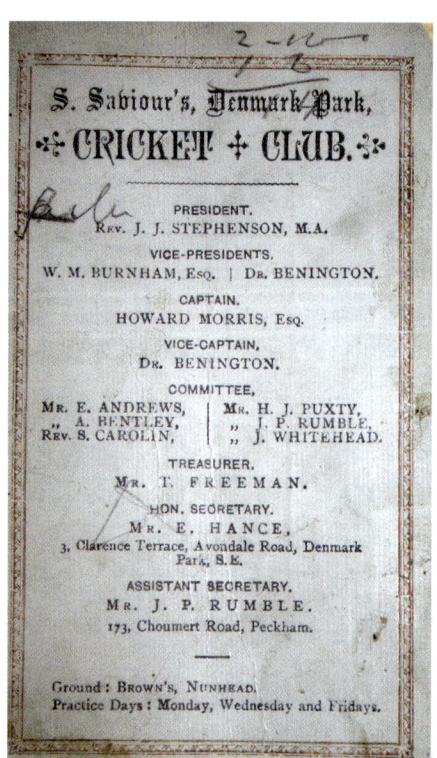

14. *St Saviour's Cricket Club fixture list 1883.* From the parish records. By courtesy of the Vicar and Churchwardens.

transitory existences. The longest-lived organisation, although not absolutely continuous throughout the period, was the cricket club: perhaps cricket, like the church itself, represented for some parishioners a connection with a rapidly receding rural past.[17]

There were two prerequisites for a flourishing social life connected with the church. One was clerical encouragement, and in particular the presence of an energetic curate willing to work with young people. The second was the availability of suitable places in which to meet. The Institute in Choumert Road was the chosen place for parties, and for the winter season of lectures and concerts, but it was small, and became increasingly booked up by activities connected with the Sunday school. In 1886 the ever-generous Francis Peek gave a house near the church, 72 Avondale Road, to provide 'healthful recreation for the young men of the parish'.[18] Known as Church Lodge, it had games rooms, a piano and a small library. But it had no large room for the bigger parish occasions, and in any case it came to an end in 1891, after a life of only five years.

What was needed was a parish or church hall, but there was no room to build one next to the church or on the Institute site. In 1891, however, the parish had a stroke of luck. The freehold of 50 Copleston Road, nearly opposite the church, came up for sale. Its tenant Henry Carrington was a leading member of the congregation, and it was probably he who suggested that the parish should buy it. It was able to do so because Peek allowed it to sell the now defunct Church Lodge and apply the proceeds to the purchase price. That alone was not enough, but the rest of the money was raised by a mortgage. In the short term Carrington would continue to live in the house, and his rent would pay the interest on the loan. In the longer term, when he and the parish were ready, he would move out, the house would be pulled down and a parish hall erected on the plot.

There, however, the matter rested for several years. Swithinbank did not give a high priority to 'entertainments', and the money to build the hall had still to be raised. It was slow to come in, despite a successful bazaar in 1894. Finally the arrival of Haslam provided the necessary impetus. Carrington vacated the house in 1900, moving to Dulwich; the fund-raising campaign reached a climax with a grand bazaar; and Church House was opened in

1902. Even so Haslam had to go for a relatively cheap option, raising the new building on the (not very good) foundations of the old. It provided a large hall or meeting room, which could be used for lectures or concerts (Haslam, with the aid of his gas-powered magic lantern, was an indefatigable lecturer), and below there were three basement rooms, suitable for bible classes or society meetings. The large garden, which stretched down to the railway line, could be used for outdoor events in summer. Haslam envisaged a whole raft of new organisations, including a Young Men's Society and a branch of the Church of England Temperance Society (which the parish had never had, although the Society was popular enough in south London). But he was not vouchsafed the time or the help necessary to realise his ambitious programme.

* * * * *

Two other institutions contributed to the rhythm of parochial life, one on a monthly and the other on a yearly cycle. The parish magazine was started by Stephenson in 1882. Already by January 1883 it had a circulation of three hundred, and in the 1890s this rose to a thousand, indicating a wider readership than the core of regular worshippers. It remained, however, under the editorial control of the vicar, who found it useful for advertising times of services, publicising other events and giving the names and addresses of officers and people to get in touch with. Stephenson had also seen the magazine as 'a means of recording Parish events, and of communicating to the people matters that cannot be dealt with in Church'. But during the Swithinbank era there was little of a secular nature in its pages, apart from regular reports of cricket and football matches in due season. There were indeed complaints that it was too 'churchy', not surprisingly when the section headed 'Parish Life' was illustrated by a view of the high altar.[19] Independent views, expressed in letters to the editor, were generally lacking, although on one occasion the committee of the cricket club wrote to complain about Swithinbank's facetious comments on its recent poor performance.

If it was not easy to voice dissent in the magazine, at least there was an opportunity at the annual vestry meeting. As we have seen, there were lively proceedings in 1885 and 1886. In 1901 Haslam's decision to drop the

Athanasian Creed from some services gave rise to a debate. But in the 1890s the vestry became a largely formal occasion at which treasurers and auditors droned through the accounts and everybody thanked everybody else for their sterling work over the previous year. Secular matters cropped up very rarely: the vestry had in any case no civil role. But the lack of a telegraph office in the parish was mentioned in 1891, and the ventilation of the parish drains in 1896.[20] Swithinbank, a blunt Yorkshireman who enjoyed a good argument, rather regretted this tameness.[21] Perhaps the underlying problem was that by this period the vestry was an antiquated and clumsy way of providing a forum for the parish. When Bishop Talbot opened Church House in 1902 he saw it partly as 'a place of conference, … where the voices of laymen could be heard…. No modern parish could be considered complete without such a meeting place.'[22] Parish councils, on which the different organisations of the parish were represented, were not unknown in the late nineteenth century; but St Saviour's had to wait until Daukes's time before it became a 'modern parish' in that sense.[23]

Although Swithinbank had a combative element in his character he was nonetheless thankful not to have a faction-ridden parish. When he left in 1899 he was glad to be able to say that 'party spirit always seemed to shrivel in the atmosphere of St Saviour's, and anyone who had tried to foster it had only courted failure and self-effacement.'[24] Party spirit may have been largely absent, but there was undoubtedly grumbling from time to time, and this had a tendency to surface in committee meetings rather than at the annual vestry. Both Stephenson and Haslam had a relaxed attitude to committees: they both thought it 'a good plan to give every one an interest in Church work by finding something for them to do.'[25] Swithinbank's perspective was a little different: he saw committees as 'a means of keeping in check the influence of particular laymen, and so preserving the supremacy of the parson'.[26] It is significant that he had most trouble with the Sunday school committee. At one point he was reduced to writing critical comments in red ink in its minute book.[27]

1. *SLP*, 23 July 1870.
2. The reverberations were felt as far away as East Dulwich.
3. Frances Knight, in *The Nineteenth-century Church and English Society* (Cambridge 1995, p5), has pointed out the dangers of describing parish life in 'narrowly liturgical and ecclesiological terms'.
4. Quoted in John D Beasley, *Peckham and Nunhead Churches*, London [1995], p82. To judge from figures quoted by Hugh McLeod (*Class and Religion*, pp301-4), the attendance at St Saviour's was higher as a proportion of the population of the parish than at churches in Peckham Rye and Camberwell as a whole.
5. For watch-night services in (greater) Southwark see Sarah Williams, 'Urban popular religion and the rites of passage', in Hugh McLeod, *European Religion in the Age of Great Cities 1830-1930*, London and New York 1995, p223.
6. For parishes with a strong missionary emphasis see, eg, David McIlhiney, *A Gentleman in Every Slum: Church of England missions in East London 1837-1914*, Pennsylvania 1988.
7. Note in the parish records, from an 1882 volume of the *Magazine* now lost.
8. There were three lay readers in 1890, five in 1893 and nine in 1896.
9. For baptisms see Sarah Williams, *op cit*, pp219-22. As for Sunday schools, it was widely recognised that they gave hard-working parents a chance to put their feet up on a Sunday afternoon, or even retire to bed together.
10. *Magazine*, Jan 1904. The numbers at St Saviour's were not extraordinary by south London standards. In 1885 the Baptist chapel in Rye Lane, Peckham claimed to have a thousand children in its Sunday school (*SLP*, 6 June 1885).
11. P73/SAV/A/04/001-2.
12. Views on when to confirm children varied. Swithinbank would put forward candidates as young as twelve (the age at which I was confirmed in 1955), but Daukes would not propose any younger than fourteen. (*Magazine*, July 1905.)
13. For lady visitors see also below, chapter 7.
14. For cliques see also below, chapter 8.
15. A register for this guild was among the parish records in 1978, but I have not seen it since.
16. London Metropolitan Archives, Acc 2831/1, Sunday school teachers' minute book 1886-99.
17. See also below, chapter 8.
18. *SLP*, 8 Oct 1887. He must have acquired the plot for 72 Avondale Road when assembling the site for the church.

19. From 1891 this illustration showed the altar candles *lit*.
20. These are references from the *Magazine*: the vestry minutes themselves omit them.
21. *Magazine*, May 1892.
22. *Ibid*, Aug 1902.
23. In the autumn of 1905 Daukes convened a kind of church council to consider the need for further remedial work on Church House. Regular PCC meetings were introduced a few years later.
24. *SLP*, 13 May 1899.
25. *Magazine*, July 1883, Mar 1901.
26. Or so, possibly tongue in cheek, he told readers of the *Magazine* (Apr 1892).
27. LMA, Acc 2831/1.

6.
WAYS AND MEANS

IT COST ABOUT a thousand pounds a year to keep the parish of St Saviour's in the manner to which it had so rapidly become accustomed. The total can be broken down approximately as follows:

	£
Clerical stipends	480
Church maintenance and services	270
Charitable and extraordinary expenses	150
Sunday school	100
Total	1,000

Nearly half the total was spent on the clergy, but this figure assumes the employment of two curates. The parish provided £330 for the vicar – £300 in seat rents and £30 in Easter offerings – but out of this he was expected to employ a curate at £150. The remaining £150 is accounted for by the second curate, for which the congregation was directly liable. The figure for maintenance includes the heating, lighting and cleaning of the church and the cost of the services; and the biggest item in connection with the services was the music. The organist was paid £50 a year, and the choirboys were paid either in cash or in kind, with books and treats. (If paid in cash they tended to be less respectable and less well-behaved.) The heading of charitable and extraordinary expenses includes regular giving through the collection to hospitals, overseas missions and so on, but also the major projects that had to be funded from time to time. St Saviour's was fortunate in that it started with a new building, with no debt on it; but thereafter the expenses gradually began to mount, with items such as a new organ or improved heating. These large items included the £1,200 that had to be raised for Church House: I have spread them out over the period in order to produce an average annual figure. Finally the Sunday school, although run mainly on voluntary labour, had certain inevitable costs. Regular expenditure, including the hire of the rooms in the Board school, came to £60, and incidentals such as the annual treat brought the total up to around £100.[1]

The parish had therefore to find large sums of money in proportion to its size – perhaps a pound a year for every adult churchgoing parishioner. To do this it had four main methods. Seat rents and offertories were the usual, and reasonably discreet, means of paying the vicar. Otherwise the principal standbys were subscriptions and money-raising events such as bazaars.

As already described, the arrangements for seat rents had been settled at the start. They are not documented (as they should have been), but it seems that it cost one pound a year to rent a seat in the designated area of the church, presumably a block in the centre of the nave. These seats were occupied by the 'solid support of the Church – ... wardens, sidesmen, auditors, organist, sub-organist, district visitors, Sunday school teachers'. The clergy liked the system because they could see from the pulpit who were in their places, and we are told that the seat-holders themselves liked to sit together with their families. 'The English mind is particularly affected by locality – we like to have a settled place of our own in Church or elsewhere.'[2]

Even in 1880 the system had its critics. The *South London Press* remarked in 1883 that seat rents were beyond the purse of 'clerks with small salaries' and 'educated artisans'; and it would of course cost four or five pounds a year to rent seats for a family, at a time when a whole house could be rented for thirty.[3] Moreover not everybody wanted to be conspicuous, especially those who were irregular in their attendance. In the 1890s seats became more difficult to let, and in 1897 the churchwardens, in the absence of the vicar who was convalescing after an illness, appealed for a 'settled support' for him. In May 1901 the wardens returned to the subject, noting 'the gradual removal from the neighbourhood of old seat-holders' and the fact that 'in this continually changing neighbourhood the newcomers do not seem to take the place of the old.' By 1903 the lettings had dropped below two hundred, and the Easter vestry, aware of a 'strong disinclination on the part of the people to pay for their seats', decided that in principle all the seats in the church should be 'free and open'.[4] The problem was to find a viable alternative, and it was not until the middle of the First World War that seat rents at St Saviour's were finally abolished.

The other, and much smaller, contribution to the vicar's income from the congregation was the Easter offertory. It seldom amounted to more than £35, less than Hospital Sunday, and in 1900, following the change of incumbent, it fell to £27.8s.4d. Some of those in the rented seats may have felt that they were already doing their bit, and those in the free seats could be stingy when the plate came round. At a bazaar in 1887 the churchwardens had a stall where they exhibited the dud coins, buttons, peppermint drops and other objects that had turned up in the collection.[5]

By the late 1890s the vicar felt that he could no longer pay for a curate out of his income, and this meant that the 'second' curate, the one directly funded by the congregation, would henceforth be the only one. Of the £150 needed, only about half could usually be raised through offertories, leaving the other half to be raised by subscription. This worked well enough on an occasional basis, but less well if resorted to more frequently, and it also exposed the financial dependence of the parish on the 'willing few'. Published subscription lists enable us to identify these people, and where they lived.

In the spring of 1884 over £132 was raised to provide a Stephenson memorial. Of this sum over half came from a mere fifteen individuals or families, giving sums of between three and ten guineas each. This little group of patrons was led by the Bristowes and the Woods. The Bristowes were a well-established family of what one might call Camberwell gentry, living in the Denmark Hill area. William Wood, a merchant, and his sister Elizabeth, who had her own means, lived in the Glebe, very near the top of the parish, and generously supported St Saviour's over many years: Miss Wood gave a total of £150 towards the cost of Church House. Other patrons came and went over the period, but their numbers remained very small. In 1890, for instance, a shortfall of £75 in the Assistant Clergy Fund was made up by six individuals.

Nearly all the small subscribers to the Stephenson memorial, those contributing less than one pound, were from within the parish. Of those who put their names down for between one and three guineas a fifth came from outside the parish (and another quarter from Copleston Road). But the five largest subscribers *all* lived outside the parish, in the Glebe, Camberwell Grove, Champion Hill and Denmark Hill. They were not in the same financial league as Francis Peek, but they represented a solid tradition of Victorian philanthropy. They saw St Saviour's as a good local cause, and had no doubt been impressed by Stephenson and saddened by his early death.[6]

As time went on this partial dependence on well-disposed people from the top of the hill became more problematic. After 1900 the middle-class exodus from this leafy district accelerated, and in 1904 Haslam was telling his flock that 'little by little we shall be obliged to recognise the fact that we must look more to our own parishioners to support their church work'.[7] Daukes saw this as more an opportunity than a threat. There were benefits in self-reliance, and (although this was not spelt out in the columns of the Magazine) there were advantages for the parson in not being beholden to a few wealthy individuals: those who paid the organist, to adapt a phrase, had a tendency to call the hymns. He soon found, however, that it was not easy to widen the basis of financial support. At the end of 1905 it was decided to raise a further £200 for work on Church House, and he proposed to do this by means of a graduated subscription. He hoped that twenty people would give £5, ten £2 and thirty £1, leaving the remaining £50 to come in small gifts from a further 220 individuals. The initial response was disappointing: he obtained eleven promises of £5, two of £2 and only nine of £1, indicating a weakness in the middle range of giving as well as the continuing existence of a small group of patrons. (He did eventually get the total up to £175, at which point he could tap the diocese for the remaining £25.)[8]

When it came to funding a really big project there was nothing to beat a good bazaar. The 1887 bazaar at the Denmark Hill Lava Skating Rink, so-called because the surface was asphalt rather than ice, helped to raise £800 for the organ fund,[9] and similar events in 1894, 1901 and 1903 produced £900 for the Church House fund. They required feats of organisation, and left the participants exhausted, but were said to provide a bonding experience for those involved. The 1901 bazaar was a three-day affair, and Haslam was able to produce three 'names' to perform the opening ceremonies. The first two were aristocratic ladies well-known in Anglican circles, but the third was a real coup, the banker Alexander Kleinwort. Kleinwort lived in a large house in the Glebe, next to the Woods, and his wife got 'many of the German residents' of that neighbourhood to come and spend their money at the stalls, despite the fact that their own church was the German Lutheran chapel near Denmark Hill station.[10] Only two things marred the success of the proceedings. The cost of hiring the hall had to be deducted from the takings, and the social tone was too exclusive for some parishioners. The articles were marked up with well-to-do lady shoppers in mind, thus deterring those such as members of the mothers' meeting who were unable to pay 'bazaar prices'.

1. The parish accounts were complicated, so much so that they needed a wise head such as that of the local bank manager to get a grip on them from time to time. These average figures have been extrapolated from a number of individual accounts which changed their form over the period. Out of a similar total of £1,100 St Peter's, Caversham, near Reading, spent £250 on church expenses, less than at St Saviour's, but £153 on educational purposes (Yeo, *Religion and Voluntary Organisations*, p156).

2. *Magazine*, Mar 1897, quoting the Magazine for Feb 1882 (now lost).

3. 3 Feb 1883.

4. *Magazine*, Apr 1900, Mar 1901, May 1902, Feb, May and Aug 1903.

5. *SLP*, 11 June 1887.

6. For the middle-class element in the congregation see also below, chapter 7.

7. *Magazine*, Apr 1904.

8. *Ibid*, Nov-Dec 1905.

9. It was remarked that the Rink made a suitably airy space for a bazaar, even if the floor was a little slippery (*SLP*, 11 June 1887).

10. *Magazine*, Apr-July 1901; *SLP*, 8 and 22 June 1901.

7.

WORSHIPPERS AND WORKERS

WHEN GEORGE ELLYATT died in 1898 he was the first layman to be honoured with a memorial in the church. A simple brass on the middle chancel step remembered him as 'a loyal worshipper and worker'.[1] This chapter considers the social composition of the congregation at St Saviour's, and looks at some of the workers who left their mark on parish life.

In the absence of a register of seat rents it is difficult to identify the core of regular worshippers, but fortunately a communicants' roll survives for Swithinbank's time. It does not give occupations, but where it gives addresses one can make a rough guess at the social level of those who knelt at the communion rail (see Table II). What is striking about the communicant body is the size of the middle-class element within it – much larger than the social composition of the Peckham Rye and Denmark Park estates would lead one to expect (see Table I).[2] This was still true in 1899, the year that Swithinbank left the parish, but there is some evidence to suggest a rapid falling-off in Haslam's time. Of twenty-six candidates presented for Confirmation in 1903, only two came from middle-class homes: the comparable figure for 1905 is four out of forty-four.[3]

For the social composition of the congregation as a whole it is necessary to turn, *faute de mieux*, to the baptismal registers. They include some families that had no on-going connection with the church, but they do give occupations; they provide evidence over the whole of our period; and they also enable comparisons to be made with other parishes. Table III suggests that the congregation was predominantly lower middle-class, which is more what one would expect from the profile of the neighbourhood. This remained true in 1901, although less conspicuously so than twenty years earlier. The number of middle-class baptisms, however, was higher than one would expect from the population of the parish, although by the late 1890s the numbers were lower than they had been in the early 1880s.

Clearly the great majority of the church's middle-class supporters must have come from outside the parish. The meaning of parish boundaries in this part of south London will be considered more fully in chapter 9, but here it can be mentioned that of 103 middle-class communicants in the years 1888-94, 41 came from Camberwell Grove, Grove Lane, Grove Park and other streets near the top of Grove Hill. Most of this area fell within St Giles's parish. In 1886 St Giles's had the poorest congregation of the parishes immediately bordering St Saviour's, and this was still true ten years later, although by then a general social decline in the district had tended to blur the difference (see Table IV). For some of the prosperous residents at the southern end of Camberwell Grove and its vicinity the social tone of St Saviour's may therefore have been more attractive than that of their own parish church.

* * * * *

The wealthiest supporters of St Saviour's, the patrons described in chapter 6, were a small group, and one that tended not to get involved with the day-to-day affairs of the parish. The only two exceptions that I have identified were J Hepburn Hastie, of Champion Park, who became a lay reader, and HM Dalston, of Grove Lane, who acted as honorary treasurer for a number of parochial funds. More typical of this group were William Wood, of the Glebe, and his sister Elizabeth, who despite their generosity to St Saviour's remained primarily attached to their own parish of St John's.[4]

Turning to the leading workers, there is no better place to start than with the churchwardens. The first vicar's warden was Walter Burnham (warden 1881-7), an advertising contractor. Originally resident in the parish, at 64

Copleston Road, he had moved to Grove Lane by 1886. He was succeeded by George Ellyatt, whose death in 1898 has already been mentioned. Ellyatt was a builder, who lived in Ivanhoe Road before translating himself to Grove Park. Clearly a committed churchman, he was active as a choirman and assistant organist as well as a churchwarden, and we are told that the archdeacon of Essex was 'an old family friend'. Swithinbank valued him for his 'outspoken and (mark that!) *direct* but always kindly advice'. Ellyatt was succeeded by AHP Dale, another Grove Park resident.[5] A bank manager, he ran the Peckham branch of the London and South-western Bank for twenty-seven years before being promoted to the City branch in 1905.[6] His financial acumen was of great value to the parish, and he also helped to smooth the transition from Swithinbank to Haslam.

The people's wardens, elected rather than chosen by the vicar, were on the whole less partisan in their churchmanship and more active in the wider community. The first, Dr Benington, was one of the few undeniably middle-class inhabitants of the Peckham Rye estate, living in a house on the corner of Copleston Road and Danby Street, but he moved before long to his practice on Denmark Hill. A public-spirited young medical practitioner, he helped to stimulate the social life of the parish in its earliest years, along with his musical wife. He was succeeded in 1885 by another doctor, Thomas Johnston, but he was warden for only two years and does not seem to have made much of an impression. Like Ellyatt he migrated from Ivanhoe Road to Grove Park.[7]

We have already briefly met Johnson's successor Edwin Gauntlett, people's warden from 1887 to 1891. He was a commuter: for many years from 1873 he was manager of a large printing business on Tower Hill, Whitehead, Morris and Co. But he also anchored himself firmly on the Peckham Rye estate: he owned Lavington Lodge, his house at 42 Copleston Road, and also acquired three other houses in the immediate vicinity. From the start of his residence he took 'a lively interest in neighbourhood as well as church affairs'. He appeared on local platforms, served in the early 1880s as a Camberwell vestryman and in the early 1900s as a Camberwell borough councillor, and for some years ran two small local building societies based at the Free Methodist schoolroom at the bottom of Danby Street. It is noticeable that between 1887 and 1891 the *South London Press* was well supplied with reports of doings at St Saviour's, and it is likely that Gauntlett was the correspondent. Although he was, as we have seen, far from being a high churchman, he was supported as warden in 1887 by what his neighbour John Lightfoot called 'the "church" party – by which he meant that section of the parishioners and the outside congregation who worshipped at and supported their church.' But he resigned after four years in office, probably in protest at Swithinbank's further moves in the direction of ritualism.[8]

Henry Carrington, Gauntlett's successor as people's warden, was by contrast a local businessman. An Essex man by birth, he had established a flourishing draper's business in Rye Lane. By the mid-1880s he was living with his family in Blenheim Grove, near his Rye Lane shop and even nearer to the church of All Saints, where for some years he was a worshipper. But in 1888 he moved to 50 Copleston Road, which, as already described, was acquired by the parish in 1891. Carrington remained there as tenant until 1900, when he moved to Dulwich, but retained his office of churchwarden until his death in 1910. I have the impression that he was not a doctrinaire churchman: he was a sociable man who enjoyed organising parish events, for some of which he would supply the drapery. In moving from All Saints' to St Saviour's he may have been attracted by the less puritan and more congenial atmosphere of the latter rather than by Swithinbank's particular brand of churchmanship. His daughters also helped with parish entertainments, and at one period ran a small private school at no 50.[9]

The churchwardens were at the top of the lay hierarchy, and were normally men of some substance and local standing.[10] But the bulk of the work was done by a different set of men, very often younger men as yet without families and still making their way in their chosen commercial or clerical careers. Swithinbank later recalled that his band of workers included higher grade civil servants, Post Office workers, numerous bank employees, both City and suburban, and representatives of the teaching and medical professions.[11] This is of course a male-dominated list, but it does include lady teachers, and even some female Post Office workers. Typical of these lower middle-class families were the Couratins, the Westrups and the Rumbles. Arthur and Paul Couratin, the sons of a clerk, both became lay readers and senior Sunday school officials, as did George Westrup from a similar background. Joseph Percy Rumble, an India Office messenger who settled at 173 Choumert Road in 1881, was another active churchman, and, like Gauntlett, became a small owner of house property in the parish. Both the Westrups and the Rumbles remained closely associated with St Saviour's well into the twentieth century.[12]

These men and women usually had addresses in the parish, and there was a tendency for them to gravitate to Copleston Road. Arthur Couratin married another Sunday school teacher, and set up house at no 66. George Westrup moved with his parents from Crofton Road (outside the parish) to 72 Copleston Road in 1894, and moved to no 90 when he married in 1900. The Heards, who became connected by marriage to the Carringtons and the Gauntletts, lived at no 28, while no 70 was the home of Joseph Harnden, a bank clerk who served variously as Sunday school teacher, vestry clerk and ruridecanal representative.

So far in this chapter the women, although forming the major part of the communicant body, have been mentioned only in passing. That is because they were excluded from all the leading lay positions. They were confined to those areas of parish life where they could draw on what were perceived to be their particular skills, arising in great part from their roles as wives and mothers. Thus they tended to be mature matrons, sometimes, one suspects, a touch more refined than their husbands, or spinsters of a certain age.[13] They arranged flowers, laundered vestments and altar cloths, sat at the piano or behind the tea urn, and set out their stalls at the grand bazaars.[14] More challengingly they were the mainstay of the Sunday school and the visiting system, and helped the vicar to run the bible classes. Miss Lymbery, of Oakhurst Grove, East Dulwich, took the class for maidservants, and Mrs Ingall, who during the week ran a small school for 'gentlemen's children' at her home in Champion Grove, presided over one for middle-class girls and women.

Perhaps the most hard-working woman in the parish during our period was Mrs Haslam. Apart from leading the parish ladies from the front she acted as her husband's clerk and diary-keeper, and for some years they denied themselves holidays together so that the parish did not grind to a halt in his absence. During his last illness she found herself dealing with a mountain of correspondence, only to find that when he died her role came to a sudden end. She had of course to vacate the Vicarage, and to leave the parish. One may imagine her feelings as she penned the briefest of farewell notes for the Magazine.

1. *Magazine*, May 1898. The brass has not survived.
2. The figures in Tables I and II are not directly comparable: the percentages in Table I represent portions of a larger total. Nevertheless the contrast is significant.
3. P73/SAV/A/04/002.
4. Miss Wood was a visitor for St John's, and left that parish £200 in her will (St John's parish magazine Mar 1886; ECE 7/1/47447/2).
5. The Chadwick estate built a number of comfortably middle-class houses on their Grove Park estate towards the end of the century.
6. *SLP*, 23 May 1905.
7. *Ibid*, 1 Aug 1885.
8. *Ibid*, 19 Feb 1898, 16 Apr 1887, 20 Nov 1880, 14 May 1881, 5 May and 24 Nov 1883. John Lightfoot, a restaurateur in London, lived at 46 Copleston Road (later occupied by the Westrup family), and, although never a churchwarden, was conspicuous in church and local affairs. His brother Joseph, a shellfishmonger, lived at no 100.
9. Emily and Louisa Carrington were confirmed at St Saviour's *before* the move to Copleston Road.
10. The churchwardens subscribed three guineas to the Stephenson fund in 1884, whereas the younger parish workers put themselves down for between five shillings and one guinea.
11. Jubilee booklet, 1931.
12. Westrup's son Jack (later Sir Jack) became assistant organist at St Saviour's, and later Heather Professor of Music at Oxford (where I encountered him once or twice). Miss Rumble was PCC secretary in the 1940s, and left 173 Choumert Road to the parish as a house for the curate. It is now the Vicarage.
13. According to Mr Carolin, one of the curates, lady visitors should be at least in their mid-twenties (*Magazine*, July 1884).
14. A report on the 1887 bazaar refers to 'a bevy of lady attendants' (*SLP*, 11 June 1887). The strategic planning of the event, however, was a male preserve.

TABLE II

ST SAVIOUR'S: SOCIAL COMPOSITION OF COMMUNICANT FAMILIES

	% 1888-94	% 1899
Middle-class	28	27
Lower middle-class and artisan	72	70.5
Labouring	0.25	2.5

Sources: roll of communicants 1888-1900 (P73/SAV/A/04/001); classification of streets in Booth's Poverty Survey (map 1889; *Streets and Population Classified*, 1892; revision 1899, see *The Streets of London*, 1997).

Note: The occupations of fathers of baptised children in 1886 (using the baptismal register for that year and the social classification adopted in chapter 2 above) were found to correlate closely with their addresses (using the Booth street classification of 1889).

	1886 (%)		1889 (%)
Middle-class	11	red streets	11
Lower middle-class and artisan	80	pink or pink-barred streets	86
Labouring	10	purple or blue	4

Fathers of baptised children are counted only once, even though more than one child from the same 'baptismal family' might be registered during the year. Baptismal families are omitted where no occupation or identifiable address is given in the register. It should also be noted that Booth does not enable one to distinguish artisan streets from middle-class ones, since his 'pink' category covers both.

TABLE III

ST SAVIOUR'S: SOCIAL COMPOSITION OF BAPTISMAL FAMILIES

	% 1881	% 1886	% 1891	% 1896	% 1901
Middle-class	16	11	12	7	8
Lower middle-class	66	53	62	48	58
Artisan	16	26	26	35	28
Labouring	2	10	0	10	6

Source: baptismal registers. (For the definitions of baptismal families and social classes see the note to Table II.)

TABLE IV

ST SAVIOUR'S AND NEIGHBOURING CHURCHES: SOCIAL COMPOSITION OF BAPTISMAL FAMILIES

% 1886

	St Saviour's	St John's	All Saints'	St Giles's
Middle-class	11	11	11	4
Lower middle-class	53	41	55	42
Artisan and labouring	36	48	34	54

% 1896

	St Saviour's	St John's	All Saints'	St Giles's
Middle-class	7	6	4	3
Lower middle-class	48	45	41	33
Artisan and labouring	45	49	55	63

Source: baptismal registers (All Saints' in parochial custody, the rest at LMA).

8.
A FRIENDLY COMMUNITY

'WE ALL', STEPHENSON told his congregation, 'know the sadness of that "Alone in London".' Swithinbank, writing in the parish magazine a few years later, was more locally specific: 'The circumstances of our parish are peculiar in this: there are so many lonely lives.'[1] They were not, of course, thinking of the committed workers described in chapter 7, but of ordinary parishioners with very limited social lives. Some valued their privacy, and 'kept themselves to themselves', but others, perhaps house-bound or with few friends in the neighbourhood, did not relish their isolation. For such people the church could provide a focus and a framework. Haslam, using a word beloved of later historians and sociologists, declared that the church should be at the centre of a 'friendly community'.[2] For Swithinbank the word probably had more of a monastic than a parochial connotation. He preferred to speak of 'the communion of saints in everyday life' as a special kind of friendship.[3]

There were three principal ways in which the clergy could encourage this friendliness. They could promote the church services themselves as a 'bonding' experience for the congregation[4]; they could discourage divisions within the congregation, particularly along class lines; and they could foster social activities that could in turn strengthen the parochial community. This chapter will look again at some of the features of parish life described in chapter 4, in order to assess how far these measures were successful at St Saviour's, and indeed how far the clergy varied in their commitment to them.

* * * * *

As we have seen, Stephenson wanted services to be 'congregational', and this seems to have been part of their attraction for those who attended them. Certainly vigorous hymn-singing is a good bonding activity. Under Swithinbank, however, the tendency was to less congregational participation, and Haslam moved to reverse the trend, asking the organist to concentrate on improving the 'ordinary part of the service', the hymns and responses. When newcomers arrived in the parish they were asked to give in their names to the clergy, but we do not know what sort of a welcome they received when they first turned up to a Sunday service. Did they worry about wearing the right clothes, or sitting in the right seats? Did they encounter what the clergy referred to and deplored as an atmosphere of 'mutual suspicion', meaning apparently suspicions about the high or low churchmanship of their neighbours in the pews? Swithinbank liked to emphasise the *family* nature of worship. 'The leading and representative men at St Saviour's are family men, who come with their families to Church.'[5] Much later Daukes recalled the 'family feeling' of the parish as a whole.[6] It was, however, precisely the lonelier people of the parish who were less likely to have families: perhaps it was hoped that they would embrace church life as a family substitute. It could also be remarked, if we are pursuing the family analogy, that the closer the family the more nearly self-sufficient, and hence the less welcoming to outsiders, it might be.

Addressing the Church Workers' Society in 1883, a visiting speaker argued that church societies should link 'more closely… together all earnest members of a congregation, so that the barrier which Society puts between classes might be broken down, and that all might feel a lively interest in the welfare of each other, and be striving together to do the Master's work.'[7] Stephenson made a similar point in one of his sermons:

> We here in Denmark Park, who desire to be neighbourly and
> to help each other as best we may, are not anxious, as some
> seem to be, to emphasise every little social distinction, and
> to keep coldly aloof on every little conventional pretext, but
> with a due regard and remembrance of each others'

> circumstances and our respective positions and responsibilities, we long to make our place something more than a mere collection of houses and ourselves something more than a mere aggregation of families casually thrown into them....[8]

These remarks from the pulpit sound more normative than descriptive, and unfortunately for Stephenson and his successors class distinctions had been built into the very fabric of church life. The seat-rent system, as we have seen, created a distinction between the better-off occupants of the rented seats and the rest of the congregation; but perhaps more serious in its social effect was the division between the church congregation as a whole and that of the little mission church-cum-Sunday school in Choumert Road. The mission services were meant to cater for those who found it harder to get to church, or who did not wish to have to consider 'the question of dress, as, unfortunately, too many do who go to church'.[9] But as the activities at the Institute developed their own social life the gap between the two congregations widened.

The topography of the parish did not help. The church, although below the railway line, really belonged to the upper end of the parish. The wealthier members of the congregation came *down* the hill to its services. The Sunday school children, on the other hand, marched *up* to the church when they attended the occasional service there. When Church House was opened the Sunday school preferred to remain where it was, and one gathers from Magazine reports that the residents of Copleston Road were rather relieved to be spared a regular Sunday invasion of two or three hundred children. As already noted, these were mainly Board School children: middle-class children, who went to private schools during the week, could attend a bible class on Sundays. When Haslam revived this class in 1903 he told Magazine readers that he 'would of course be glad to welcome friends *or servants* [my italics] who may come with the young people'.[10]

One important aspect of neighbourliness was looking out for and looking after those who needed help and support, but even this area of parish life was constrained by social conventions. In the lower part of the parish cases of need or distress were dealt with by the vicar and the lady visitors, although members of the Mothers' Meeting no doubt had their own networks.[11] In Copleston Road neighbours rallied round in a rather different way. In 1903 AH Lewis, of 102 Copleston Road, a draper by occupation and a pillar of the church as sidesman and sacristan, died suddenly 'in a tram car on his way to business'. A subscription of £75 was raised for his wife and family, plus £5 for a memorial tablet. Young Wilfrid Lewis was nominated for a place at the Warehousemen's, Clerks' and Drapers' School at Purley, and Mrs Lewis continued to receive tactful support from those who bought her home-made marmalade and sent their children to her for piano lessons.[12]

* * * * *

It was not only class that could create divisions. A common pitfall of parish life was the tendency to develop a culture of insiders and outsiders, and the consequent creation of what clergy sometimes referred to as 'cliques'. Although Swithinbank did not like cliques his policy of fostering a core of 'real St Saviour's people' had precisely that effect. The Guild, by the time Haslam arrived, had become 'limited and somewhat exclusive': it represented 'only some of our communicants', many of them living 'long distances away'.[13] Even in Stephenson's time another division had emerged, this time along lines of gender. In August 1883 there was some discussion of the relative roles of the Guild and the Church Workers' Society, the former having a mainly female membership and the latter one that was exclusively male. The chosen solution, however, was not to mix them up but to make the ordinary meetings of the Guild entirely female. (Later, though not until November 1897, women *were* admitted to the CWS.)

Opinion was divided when it came to the amount of secular activity that should take place under the auspices of the church. Stephenson welcomed lay initiatives, even when the help offered was 'purely secular, and was rendered in many cases by those who have not yet seen their way to undertaking any church work.' Thus when the cricket club was formed in 1882 he devoted part of a sermon to welcoming it, commending it as a healthy form of exercise but hoping also that it would become 'as distinct an agency for good in this parish as the Choir, or the Guild, or the Sunday

School', and that it would 'serve to draw those who worship in this Church to friendly and cordial sociality.'[14] Swithinbank was predictably cooler in his attitude to extramural activities. He did not object when the Guild had an outing to St Alban's Abbey, or when the Church Workers opened a meeting with 'tea, coffee and a chat' before listening to an address from the curate on 'Prayers for the Departed'. He even encouraged the occasional parish party or conversazione, appealing beforehand for 'a full and hearty gathering, freed from exclusiveness or settiness social or congregational'. But his tolerance had its limits. 'It is funny', he wrote in July 1897, 'to hear newcomers to the parish wonder why so little is "going on" in the entertainment line. Our danger is lest we have too much.'[15] Haslam found a definite lack of *esprit de corps* in the parish. 'We need more of the social element', he wrote in December 1900: 'this is generally acknowledged.' Daukes took a more cautious view. He regarded a young men's club as 'essential for a healthy Christian parish'. But the tail should not wag the dog. 'I do not believe in building up a Church from a Club', he said, 'but in forming a Club out of a Church.'[16]

As we have seen, it did not prove easy to sustain social and cultural organisations at St Saviour's, and Haslam's own efforts in that sphere did not bear the fruit that he had hoped. Again, the trouble was partly the diverging tastes of different social groups. The Copleston Road community did its bit in laying on jolly evenings at the Institute, but it also had its own, less inclusive leisure activities. Especially in Swithinbank's time there were groups that met in private houses – a chess club, a Shakespeare Society, said to have been started by the vicar himself, and a Champion Hill Browning Circle, founded by the curate Alan Gordon Smith and described in the Magazine as 'a small society into which much of the wisdom of the parish is condensed'.[17] Swithinbank was not anti-culture: he simply preferred the middle-class variety.

An organised sport like cricket was supposed to help break down class barriers, but unfortunately money also came into it. It cost half a guinea a year to join the cricket club at St Saviour's, and on top of that there were the expenses of the clothes and equipment, travel to away fixtures and the annual dinner. When a tennis club was formed in 1892 it was welcomed as including ladies; but the costs of hiring courts on the ground below Champion Hill made it necessary to fix the subscription at a guinea for the men and fifteen shillings for the women.[18] The young men's club at Church Lodge had charged ten shillings a year, and this may have been one of the reasons for its closure in 1891. In contrast the subscription for Haslam's new literary and scientific society at Church House was fixed at the 'purposely low' figure of half-a-crown for both men and women. St Saviour's was taking its first tentative steps into the twentieth century.

1. Stephenson, *Sermons*, p108; *Magazine*, Oct 1890.

2. *Magazine*, Dec 1903.

3. *SLP*, 13 May 1899.

4. Sociologists, discussing the nature and dynamics of social organisations, have made a useful (though not watertight) distinction between 'bonding' activities, those that consolidate and strengthen reciprocal ties within an organisation, and 'bridging' activities, those that reach out to elements in the wider community. (See Robert D Putnam, *Bowling Alone: the collapse and revival of American community*, New York and London 2000, p22 and n20, quoting Ross Gittell and Avis Vidal, *Community Organising: building social capital as a development strategy*, Thousand Oaks, California 1998, p8.) Bridging activities at St Saviour's are considered in Part III below.

5. *Magazine*, May 1898.

6. Jubilee booklet.

7. *Magazine*, July 1883.

8. Stephenson, *Sermons*, p220.

9. *Magazine*, Jan 1903.

10. *Ibid*, Feb 1903. At St Philip's, Kennington the private school children would not mix with the Board school children (Cox, *English Churches in a Secular Society*, p63).

11. For charitable work see also below, chapter 13.

12. *Magazine*, Feb-Apr 1903, May 1904.

13. *Ibid*, Nov 1899.

14. Stephenson, *Sermons*, pp211-12. At the annual dinner of the Choumert Cricket Club at the Victoria public house the chairman remarked that 'cricket clubs had a tendency to create and cement friendships, as there was no distinction on the field, and each one tried in thorough good feeling to do his best.' (*SLP*, 12 Oct 1878.)

15. *Magazine*, June and Dec 1892, Dec 1898.

16. *Ibid*, Oct 1905.

17. The Browning Circle does not seem to have survived Gordon Smith's departure, but the chess club and Shakespeare Society were still going in the early twentieth century (*Magazine*, Nov 1905).

18. *Magazine*, Feb 1892.

PART III
CONNECTIONS

9.
'IMAGINARY LINES': THE BOUNDARIES OF THE PARISH

AS WE SAW in chapter 3, the Ecclesiastical Commissioners took great pains in 1881 to settle and describe the boundaries of the new parish. Where possible they followed existing features of the landscape, such as the course of Cut-throat Lane, an ancient local boundary that had previously marked the northern limit of St John's parish. In the Bellenden Road area, on the other hand, they had to draw 'imaginary lines' down the middle of the streets. Between the southern ends of Oglander and Copleston Roads the boundary could not even follow the middle of a street, since the imaginary line was drawn straight across a small area of still unbuilt-up land. To mark this section the Commissioners decided that two boundary stones should be erected, one at either end of it. The stones were to be inscribed 'CH StS DC', for Champion Hill St Saviour's District Chapelry, a cryptic message that may have puzzled those who came upon it at the end of one of the roads in question.[1]

This insistence on precise boundaries, as if the Commissioners were defining a plot of land in a conveyance, may seem old-fashioned in the 1880s. St Saviour's, after all, could not levy rates or tithes on its land: for such purposes it was still part of the old parish of Camberwell. But it remained important to ensure that there was no debatable territory between one parish and the next. Successive incumbents of St Saviour's may not have carried in their heads a map of exactly where the imaginary lines ran, but they needed to be quite clear whether individuals lived inside or outside the parish. 'Parishioners have a claim upon the free ministrations of their Clergy,' the vicar reminded readers of the Magazine, 'whether they come to Church or not.' They could ask him to baptise them and to marry them: in the latter case there was in fact a legal residence requirement. Had St Saviour's possessed a churchyard they could have asked him to bury them there as well. The vicar also needed to know the total number of souls for whom he was responsible. This calculation had of course been a key factor in the formation of the district in the first place, and later on it could affect, for instance, whether he was entitled to a grant towards the cost of an additional curate.[2]

The vicar was, at least in the early days of the parish, far from being the only one to be familiar with where its boundaries lay. The vestry meetings of the mid-1880s, attended by the churchwardens and other leading laymen, debated the voting rights of non-residents, and the non-residents themselves had made a considered decision to support a place of worship that was not their own parish church. It was the job of the lady visitors to cover the whole parish, street by street, and if in doubt as to whether a street or part of a street was in the parish they could refer to a map hanging just inside the west door of the church. (It survives today, somewhat damaged by drawing pins.) The Magazine that these ladies distributed originally cost one penny for parishioners and twopence for non-parishioners. And as for the inhabitants of the lower part of the parish, amongst whom the visitors did much of their work, there may have been a consciousness, even if a residual one, that belonging to the parish might be useful when it came to claiming help from charitable funds.[3] More generally the somewhat isolated nature of the suburb, with its dead-end streets, and the fact that the boundaries of the parish and the suburb so nearly coincided, may have helped to reinforce a sense of parochial consciousness.

By 1905, however, this consciousness had weakened. Later vestry meetings did not revisit the residence question, and for most of Haslam's ministry neither churchwarden lived in the parish. In 1896 the tariff for the Magazine was changed: henceforward the normal charge was to be twopence, but mission people and members of the Mothers' Meeting could have it for a penny. By the turn of the century parish charity was becoming less important, with the growth of other forms of relief. And the boundaries of the Peckham Rye and Denmark Park estates were less fresh in people's minds. In 1903-5 those boundaries were in any case broken through, when Oglander, Bellenden and Copleston Roads were linked with Grove Vale. It was probably then that the two boundary stones so carefully placed by Stephenson disappeared.

    The attitudes and policies of the incumbents themselves played a part in this process. Stephenson disapproved of those who, in modern parlance, shopped around – those who went to one church one Sunday and another the next. 'Your life lacks completeness', he told them: 'you forget the power of association: you seem – to me at least – to fall short of the full meaning of the word – home.'[4] But, the parish being structured as it was, he was unlikely to discourage those who *regularly* attended his church rather than that of their own parish. Swithinbank was even more disapproving of 'those rovers who will ruin their Church by going here one Sunday and somewhere else the next, or who (worse still because disloyal) divide their attention between Church and Chapel.'[5] Years later, however, he recalled that his congregation had been swelled by 'vigorous recruits … after upsets in other parishes, notably one by New Cross and another in a square in Walworth.'[6] The Magazine for January 1890 spelt out the accessibility of the church from the nearest means of public transport, and in November 1898 it was announced that bicycle racks would be put up outside the church, 'since many of our people come from afar.' By October 1903 Haslam could write that 'parish boundaries don't mean much, people go where they like to Church, and in London all churches are surrounded by the same vast population within a few minutes' walk.' None of these incumbents appears to have followed the custom of beating the bounds, as was done annually at St Clement's for half a century.[7]

* * * * *

When Haslam wrote that Londoners had a choice of which church to attend he was doing no more than stating the fact. A more difficult question is on what grounds the choice was made in individual cases. One could support one's parish church because it *was* one's parish church; or one could choose another church because one liked the services, the preaching, the kind of churchmanship or the social *milieu*. But distance and convenience also mattered. The church that met all one's requirements might be too far away to make it practicable as a regular choice. A further look at baptismal registers may, despite their drawbacks as evidence, throw a little more light on this.

Table V counts the families that had a child or children baptised at St Saviour's at various dates between 1881 and 1904, and calculates the proportion that came from (a) within the parish and (b) from a distance of half a mile or less from the church. It suggests that there was a fall in the proportion of intra-parochial baptisms over the period, from around 80% under Stephenson to 60-65% under Swithinbank and to less than 60% in Haslam's last years. This would be consonant with the decline in parochial consciousness suggested above, but even under Haslam the percentage was still over fifty. The percentages, however, for those coming from half a mile away or less are higher – over 90% in the Stephenson era – suggesting that in many cases parents were choosing their *local* church rather than their *parish* church. The distance of half a mile as the Victorian crow flew equates roughly with Haslam's 'few minutes' walk'. If you were very choosy you might commit yourself to a longer journey, possibly involving a tram or bus ride, but for the majority it seems that a pleasant Sunday walk was part of the church-going experience. Map III shows the relevant parish boundaries, and superimposes on them circles of half a mile in radius from each church.

But what if there was more than one church within comfortable walking distance? Table VI compares, for the year 1896, the baptismal figures for St Saviour's with those for three neighbouring churches with which it shared a parish boundary. This suggests that there were two main topographical factors affecting the extent to which a church's hinterland corresponded with the area of its parish. One, fairly obviously, was the size of the parish: in a large parish most if not all the parishioners living half a mile from the church would be within the parish, but for some living near the boundary a neighbouring parish church might be nearer than their own. This assumes,

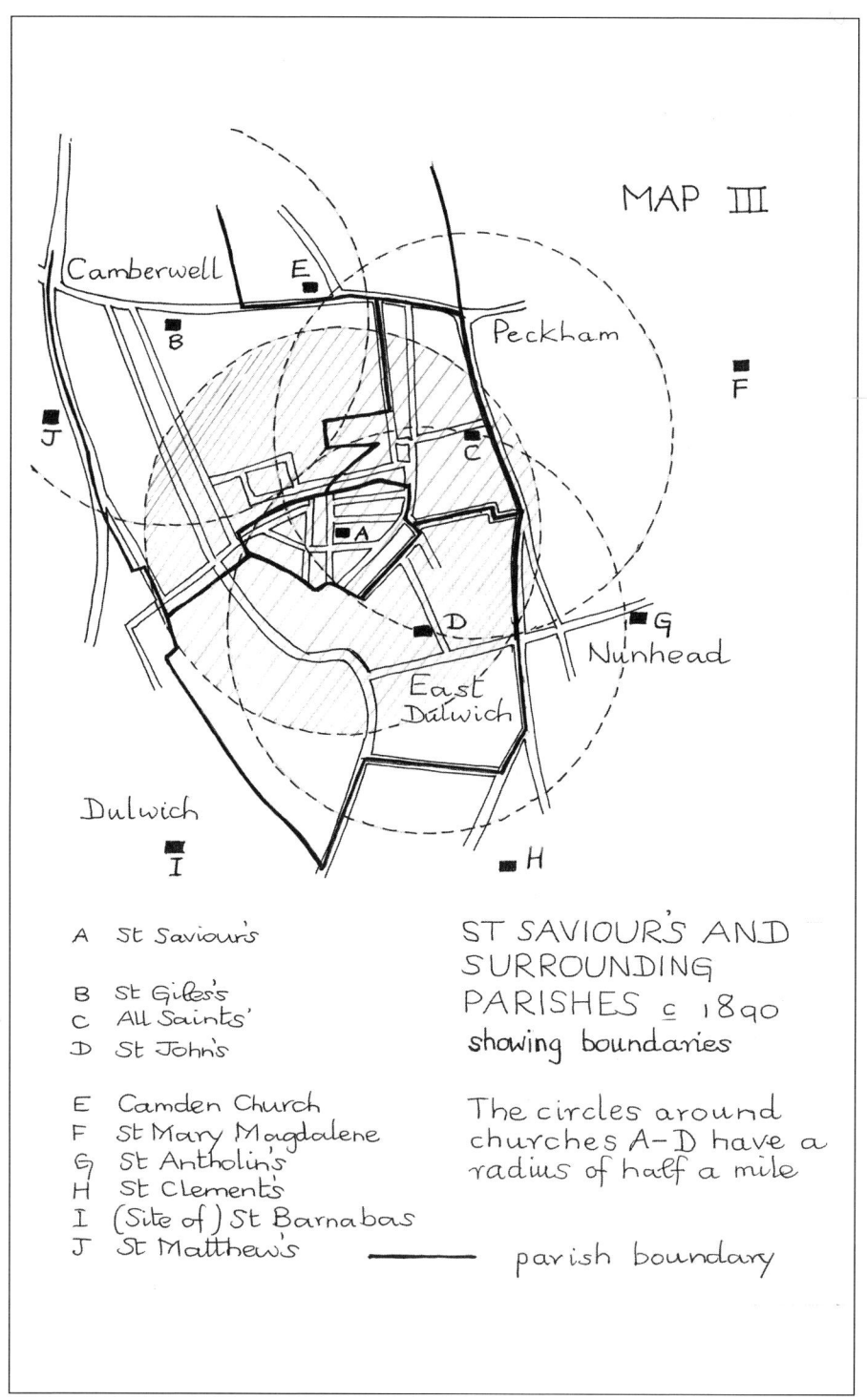

however, that the church was sited at or near the centre of its parish. If it lay near the edge the configuration would be different, with more people crossing a boundary to reach their nearest church. St Saviour's was fairly well placed in the middle of its parish, but the parish was a small one. This may explain why the percentage of intra-parochial baptisms was higher at St John's. There the church was reasonably central, but the parish was larger. All Saints', on the other hand, had an odd-shaped parish, with the church virtually on its eastern boundary. This may account for its unusually low percentage of baptisms from within the parish. A contributory factor both at All Saints' and also at St Giles's, another church with a low percentage in the table, may have been their accessibility by public transport. All Saints' was opposite Peckham Rye station, whilst St Giles's was close to one of the great transport hubs of south London.

Somewhat unusually, the inhabitants of Lyndhurst Road, a street to the north of St Saviour's parish and just south of Peckham Road, were within a reasonable distance of no less than four churches, St Giles's, All Saints', St Saviour's and Camden Church (on the north side of Peckham Road). The boundary between the parishes of the first two went down the middle of the street. (When All Saints' was set up its first incumbent had hoped to include more of this partly middle-class area in his parish, but had been fought off by the vicar of St Giles's, supported by the bishop.)[8] To judge by baptismal registers for 1886 the residents of Lyndhurst Road spread their favours. One family took their child to St Giles's, another to All Saints', and a third to St Saviour's. Camden was in fact the nearest of all, but it and its relatively poor congregation belonged definitely to *north* Peckham, so may have had less appeal to Lyndhurst Road parents.

Where a family crossed a parish boundary on its way to church, one parish's gain was of course another's loss. Table VII analyses the border traffic between St Saviour's and its three neighbours. The first two years in the table are both untypical. In 1881 some parishioners were still adhering to the churches that they had attended before St Saviour's had been built. (In 1880 twenty-one families from the future parish had had children baptised at St John's, and a further six had gone to All Saints'.) The figures for baptisms in 1886 are very high, perhaps the result of a campaign by Swithinbank.

Thereafter, however, the figures are both small and evenly balanced, suggesting that they were not likely to cause a great deal of friction or resentment between neighbouring incumbents.

Table VII suggests that brands of churchmanship were not a major factor in choosing a church for a baptism, however important it may have been to some members of the regular congregation. In the 1890s there was only a small interchange of baptismal renegades between St Saviour's and All Saints', despite the fact that at this period the former was quite High and the latter very Low. In the same period, however, St Saviour's did pick up a few baptisms from both St John's and St Giles's. Perhaps the social factors discussed in chapter 7 came into play here, although the totals are too small to be significant. The social composition of the congregations at St Saviour's and All Saints' seems to have been similar (see table IV), whereas both St John's and St Giles's included more artisan and labouring elements.

1. ECE/7/1/59883.

2. Some of these factors are still relevant today (*ex inf* the Revd Dianna Gwilliams).

3. In 1898 the vicar of Holy Trinity, Selhurst (near Croydon) commented that parish boundaries were largely ignored 'except as regards the poor and that mainly for relief purposes' (Morris, *Religion and Urban change*, p70). For the Poor Laws and parochial settlement see Snell, *Parish and Belonging*; and for parochial charity at St Saviour's see below, chapter 13.

4. *Sermons*, pp218-19.

5. *Magazine*, Apr 1890.

6. Jubilee booklet, 1931. Swithinbank was probably referring to the famous cases of St James's, Hatcham and St Paul's, Lorrimore Square, but it is hard to corroborate this. Thomas Bunce, the sacristan at St Saviour's who used to *walk* to the early Sunday service from New Cross (*Magazine*, Nov 1891), may have been one of the Hatcham refugees. (For the Hatcham case see Nigel Yates, *Anglican Ritualism*, pp254-6; James Bentley, *Ritualism and Politics in Victorian Britain: the attempt to legislate for belief*, Oxford 1978, pp100-2.) Some of those who left St Paul's for St Agnes's, Kennington Park appear later to have attended St Saviour's when they moved out to the leafier suburbs (*A Memorial of S Saviour's Denmark Park: some recent sermons, with an introduction by the Rev T Birkett Foster, vicar of S Agnes, Kennington Park, and an appendix upon work at S Saviour's for the young*, June 1894).

7. *History* of St Clement's, East Dulwich [1932]. The civil parish of Camberwell was still beating its bounds in the 1870s (Olney, 'Boundaries and landmarks: the case of Champion Hill and the manor of Dulwich', *Camberwell Quarterly*, no 159, winter 2008/9, p13).

8. ECE 7/1/35240/1.

TABLE V

ST SAVIOUR'S: RESIDENCE OF BAPTISMAL FAMILIES

	Number of families	% within parish	% within half a mile
1881	60	90	93
1882	71	66	93
1883	66	76	95
1884	78	53	83
1885	32	60	82
1886	104	62.5	87
1891	53	64	89
1896	52	66	87
1901	54	65	85
1902	47	74	90
1903	47	55	79
1904	27	59	78

Source: baptismal registers.

TABLE VI

ST SAVIOUR'S AND NEIGHBOURING CHURCHES: RESIDENCE OF BAPTISMAL FAMILIES 1896

	% within parish	% within half a mile
St Saviour's	66	86
St John's	79	87
All Saints'	37	78
St Giles's[1]	71	73

Source: baptismal registers.

1. Excluding baptisms by the workhouse chaplain.

TABLE VII

ST SAVIOUR'S (BAPTISMAL FAMILIES): GAINS FROM AND LOSSES TO NEIGHBOURING PARISHES

	1881	1886	1891	1896	1901
St John's					
Gains from	2	10	6	4	6
Losses to	5	4	1	4	3
All Saints'					
Gains from	1	9	3	4	2
Losses to	8	4	3	4	2
St Giles's					
Gains from	1	8	4	2	4
Losses to	1	0	2	2	1

Sources: baptismal registers.

10.
ST SAVIOUR'S AND THE CHURCH IN SOUTH LONDON

WHEN BISHOP TALBOT came to take a Confirmation at St Saviour's in June 1901 he arrived late: his coachman had lost the way.[1] One cannot blame him: the topography of the parish was confusing, as it still is. But the event symbolised the at times uncertain connection between the parish and the larger ecclesiastical organisation of which it was a part.

Episcopal visits were rare. Bishop Thorold had a personal connection with the parish in its early days, and Bishop Talbot knew Haslam, but Swithinbank lacked both friends in high places and a local south London background. He relied to some extent, however, on old Oxford contacts such RL Ottley, sometime Principal of Pusey House and Canon of Christ Church.[2] On a more local level, however, it was not uncommon for St Saviour's to have guest preachers, especially at major festivals or during Advent and Holy Week. During an interregnum, as in 1884, 1899 and again in 1904, special arrangements had to be made to provide the necessary cover.

Conversely there were times when the vicar left the parish to preach or officiate elsewhere. Stephenson, had he lived, would no doubt have been in increasing demand. Swithinbank did not set so much store by preaching, or 'outreach' generally. But Haslam was frequently out and about, doing the bishop's bidding in the diocese at large. October was the principal month for missionary forays, which might take him anywhere from Wandsworth down to Limpsfield.[3]

These were *ad hoc* events. It is harder to assess the regular relationship between parish and diocese. The diocese of Rochester, as reconfigured in 1877, never worked very well. Its cathedral was not in a central position, and not easily accessible by train from south London. Swithinbank and Haslam attended diocesan conferences, but parish visits to Rochester may have been limited to one trip by the Guild in 1891.[4] By the early 1890s, however, plans were already in motion that led to the creation of a new diocese of Southwark in 1905. Between 1889 and 1897 the church of St Saviour's Southwark was restored and enlarged as a cathedral-in-waiting, and the archdeacon of Southwark became a suffragan bishop. The Bishop's College moved from Rochester to Southwark in 1897, in time for it to provide a locum when Swithinbank took a much-needed summer holiday that year, and the College also came to the aid of the parish during the interregnum in September 1904.[5]

More locally one might expect St Saviour's to have had close ties with its mother church of St John's. In fact contacts seem to have been quite frequent to start with, but then to have dwindled during the Swithinbank era.[6] In the Maxted Road/Oglander Road area there could have been opportunities for the two parishes to work together, since the boundary was a somewhat porous one, but such does not seem to have been the case. Indeed St John's opened a mission room in Maxted Road in 1883, only a stone's-throw from the parish boundary and not four hundred yards from the mission room in Choumert Road. Under WJ Strickland, vicar of St John's from 1888 to 1900, 'what may be called this aggressive movement' led to the opening of an iron church on the corner of Waghorn Street in 1892. It seems, however, that there were closer relations between Strickland's successor Arthur Eglinton (1901-9) and Daukes.[7]

The old parish church of St Giles, Camberwell had been rebuilt on a grand scale after a fire in the early 1840s, but this was followed by a period of blight during which it failed to develop a role as a kind of minster church for the area of its ancient parish. The incumbent was an absentee for many years: a bankrupt, he could at one time be contacted only via his solicitor.[8] The fortunes of St Giles's revived from 1880 onwards under the Revd FF Kelly, but by then the parish had been much reduced in size, and what was left was becoming increasingly commercial rather than 'residential'.[9] St Saviour's was in the rural deanery of Camberwell, and from time to time sent representatives to ruridecanal conferences, but it is unclear what effect that form of contact had on the life of the parish.[10] St Saviour's also sent its choir to St Giles's in December 1895 to help welcome the new bishop of Rochester to south London, but the service was held there, one presumes, because the restoration work on St Saviour's, Southwark was still in progress.[11]

Finally, to complete the picture of a parish that was ecclesiastically somewhat isolated, it can be noted that it had few if any parish organisations that were affiliated to diocesan or national structures. It had no Band of Hope, and for most of the period no branch of the Church of England Temperance Society. The development of the Mothers' Meeting into a branch of the Mothers' Union and the creation of troops of scouts and guides still lay in the future in 1905. St Saviour's was, however, host for a number of years to a monthly service for the deaf and dumb. Three or four attended from the parish or immediate neighbourhood, but the rest – and numbers could reach fifty – came from a wide area, making St Saviour's in this respect 'unique among the Churches of South London'.[12]

1. *Magazine*, June 1901.
2. Ottley did not visit the parish in Haslam's time, but came again in January 1905.
3. *Magazine*, Oct 1899, Oct 1900, Oct-Nov 1903.
4. *Ibid*, July 1901; Mrs Jas A Heaton, *Origins of the Diocese of Southwark*.
5. One should also note the contribution of £200 from the Rochester Diocesan Society towards the cost of Church House.
6. St John's parish magazine for 1885-6 (in parish custody) has only two references to St Saviour's that I could find. One is to a cricket match. The other is to a local branch of the Church Defence Union to which St Saviour's was attached, but which met at St Clement's rather than St John's.
7. Parish histories by WJA Hahn [1951], p74, and Mary Boast 1991, p15. Hahn (p41) refers to Daukes as 'our good neighbour at St Saviour's'.
8. Church Commissioners' records, ECE/7/112140/1.
9. *Illustrated London News*, 29 June 1900.
10. But for a more positive view of ruridecanal gatherings see Morris, *Religion and Urban Change*, pp68-9.
11. *SLP*, 7 Dec 1895.
12. *Magazine*, Jan and July 1897, Aug 1905.

11.
OUR DISSENTING BRETHREN

SOUTH LONDON, WITH its substantial populations of clerks and artisans, was fertile ground for the spread of nonconformity, especially where the Anglican presence was weak.[1] Peckham in the first half of the nineteenth century had more or less flourishing congregations of Independents (later Congregationalists), Quakers, Baptists and Wesleyan Methodists.[2] Later the nonconformists moved out to colonise the newer suburbs, the Congregationalists establishing themselves in Linden Grove (on the Nunhead side of Peckham Rye), Barry Road and East Dulwich Grove, the Baptists at the northern end of Peckham Rye and in Lordship Lane, and the Wesleyans in Barry Road. Smaller congregations included the Roman Catholics in Lordship Lane, the Primitive Methodists in Crystal Palace Road and the Scottish Presbyterians on East Dulwich Road.

Of most interest, however, to this study are two denominations that acquired a presence on the Peckham Rye estate, the Unitarians in Avondale Road and the Free Methodists in Bellenden Road.[3] Both arrived before St Saviour's was even at the planning stage, although the church beat the chapels to it when it came to erecting a permanent building. The Unitarians were first in the field, when their small Peckham congregation found a site at the lower end of Avondale Road in 1875. At this date there were many more empty plots around it than completed houses, but the promoters were confident that 'ere long the Chapel will be surrounded by a populous neighbourhood'. The site, together with the iron chapel that soon appeared on it, cost £630, a large sum for a congregation composed mainly of 'people of small means', but help came from 'wealthier Unitarian friends' at a distance, and the London district Unitarian Society chipped in with two donations of £25.[4] A supporter gave an adjacent site with a frontage on Bellenden Road, on which a school room-cum-lecture room was erected in 1881, and the following year a permanent chapel building, in the 'early Gothic style', replaced the tin tabernacle on the original site.

Under their long-serving first pastor, George Carter, the chapel built up a small but loyal following and a lively social life. It had a Sunday school, of course, but also temperance organisations, a literary society and even a ladies' gymnasium run by the minister's daughter. Carter himself was active in local affairs: he took a particular interest in the nearby Bellenden Road Board school and in the evening school movement. He had a core of middle-class supporters, but was also anxious to reach out to working-class people. In the spring of 1883, for instance, a series of popular services attracted 'an audience made up mainly of the working classes, for whom the regular congregation had vacated their seats'.[5] Although not aggressively sectarian the Unitarians were staunchly Liberal. One of the pillars of the Avondale Road chapel, JC Fabritius of Barry Road, became treasurer of the constituency Liberal association; and another friend was Sir JC Lawrence, Liberal MP for Lambeth from 1868 to 1885.

The Free Methodists established themselves in a rather similar way. They acquired a prominent site, on the corner of Bellenden Road and Danby Street, in 1876, erected a school room in 1877, and finally, after making do with a temporary iron building for several years, put up a rather imposing chapel in the 'Romanesque style' in 1884-5. The Free Methodists, however, had fewer wealthy supporters than the Unitarians, and they were also more militant. In 1877 their minister designate claimed that 'one of the most vital powers they possessed was that of aggressiveness', and their Peckham Rye chapel was seen as part of a missionary campaign in a district in which they had few pre-existing followers.[6] Like the Unitarians, however, they enriched the social life of the neighbourhood. They too had a Sunday school, and supported the temperance movement. They had musical events (the organist lived in Copleston Road), and for many years the Peckham Tonic-Sol-fa Choir, which built up a much more than local reputation, was based in the schoolroom. But there were underlying problems and weaknesses. The early years had been difficult, and the initial debts incurred for the site and the buildings remained a millstone.[7] There were regular changes of minister, no doubt in accordance with connexional policy but resulting in a lack of continuity, and some ministers were less of a success than others. Eventually, after mounting financial and organisational problems, the chapel was sold – to the congregation from Hanover Congregational Chapel in Peckham – in 1920.

A key factor in the difficulties and eventual failure of the chapel may have been an absence of middle-class support. Chapel records have not survived, but a list of stall-holders at a bazaar in June 1892 suggests that the leading members of the congregation were lower middle-class, and drawn from Camberwell, Peckham and East Dulwich as well as the immediate vicinity.[8] The membership as a whole would probably have had a fair admixture of artisans and craftsmen from the local streets, and perhaps some of the shopkeepers of the Bellenden Road area. Certainly the failure of St Saviour's to recruit many artisans and shopkeepers left an open field for the nonconformists.[9]

* * * * *

More important, however, than the social distinctions between Church and Chapel were the cultural ones.[10] The nonconformists were a people apart from, and independent of, the Established Church, and this separateness, although beginning to weaken, was still palpable in the late nineteenth century.[11] The organisational structures of the nonconformists were, of course, less priest-dominated, but also more membership-centred. As one historian has written, 'To the church one "went", the chapel one "joined"'.[12] And politics, especially the politics of education, still presented clear divisions between Church and Dissent. If dissenters felt superior to churchmen, their disdain was reciprocated. Bishop Copleston, after whom Copleston Road was presumably named, denounced nonconformity as 'a sin and an error …, a conspiracy against the State'. Some incumbents affected to be ignorant of the very existence of chapels in their parishes.[13]

These attitudes were reflected all too clearly at St Saviour's. Readers of the parish magazine could search in vain for any reference to the two chapels in the parish. When the vicar preached he never referred to specific denominations or chapels, but only to 'our dissenting brethren', and then mainly in the context of controversy rather than co-operation. During the general election of 1892 Swithinbank made a virtue of non-partisanship – 'Some of our best friends are Radicals' – but then attacked the partisanship of "our dissenting brethren" (this time in inverted commas).[14]

This picture should, however, be modified in two respects. Firstly, the vicar could not ignore the existence of the Bellenden Road Board school, a major local institution that made a certain degree of cross-denominational contact inevitable.[15] Secondly, the blinkered attitude of the vicar was not shared by every member of his congregation. Edwin Gauntlett, for instance, used the Danby Street schoolroom for his building society meetings, and did not mind appearing on local nonconformist platforms. And who was the Mrs Gauntlett who assisted at the Free Methodist chapel bazaar in 1890? Could it have been the churchwarden's wife?[16]

1. Hugh McLeod, *Class and Religion in the Victorian City*, London 1974, pp144, 301-4.
2. John D Beasley, *Peckham and Nunhead Churches*.
3. The Wesleyans bought a site on the corner of Bromar and Grove Hill Roads, but (no doubt to the relief of successive vicars, who lived directly opposite) it was never used, and was re-sold for housing in the late 1890s.
4. *Avondale Road Chapel, South Camberwell*, [1876] (Southwark Local History Library, P288).
5. *SLP*, 24 Feb 1883.
6. Foundation stones for the schoolroom were laid by young ladies representing other societies. (*SLP*, 26 Apr 1877.) There were altogether only about fifteen Free Methodist chapels in the whole of south London at this date.
7. *SLP*, 17 Feb 1893, 7 Nov 1903.
8. *Ibid*, 18 June 1892.
9. See also McLeod, *Class and Religion*, p13; McLeod, 'White Collar Values and the Role of Religion', in Geoffrey Crossick, ed, *The Lower Middle Class in Britain 1870-1914*, London 1977, pp61-88; Cox, *English Churches in a Secular Society*, pp30-3.
10. See also SJD Green, *Religion in the Age of Decline: organisation and experience in industrial Yorkshire 1870-1920*, Cambridge 1996, p25n; Cox, *op cit*, p130.
11. Morris, *Religion and Urban Change*, pp294-301, 312ff.
12. ER Wickham, *Church and People in an Industrial City*, 1957, p141, quoted by Clyde Binfield in McLeod, ed, *European Religion in the Age of Great Cities*, p210.
13. Chris Brooks and Andrew Saint, eds, *The Victorian Church: architecture and society*, Manchester 1995, p128; Cox, *op cit*, p259.
14. *Magazine*, Feb and Aug 1892.
15. For education see below, chapter 12.
16. *SLP*, 17 May 1890.

12.
EDUCATION

THE SCHOOL BOARD for London was established under the Education Act of 1870, and in accordance with the Act the religious teaching in its schools was to be non-denominational and bible-based. We have seen how Francis Peek became a member of the Board, representing the City: he also gave the large sum of ten thousand pounds to be spent on bibles as prizes for Board school pupils.[1]

Unfortunately the Act gave rise to sectarian controversy from the start, and at local level this was fuelled by the elections for Board members. Neither Swithinbank nor Haslam hesitated to become involved in these contests. In 1892 a body of St Saviour's people was formed to canvass the parish in favour of the local Church candidate, 'in response to an invitation from the pulpit'. In 1904 Haslam was anxious to support the Church party at the elections for London County Councillors, the LCC having taken over the powers of the School Board under the Education Act of 1902. Since the opposition was busy enough, he wrote in the Magazine, 'we cannot afford to stand still'.[2] As for the 'opposition', a newly arrived minister at the Bellenden Road Free Methodist chapel was welcomed in September 1905 by a prominent local politician as 'a political parson' who would speak out strongly for the abolition of the (Conservative) Act of 1902.[3]

When, however, it came to the management of individual schools the situation was often less confrontational. When a committee of management was formed for the newly-opened Bellenden Road Board school in 1877 it had a nonconformist and Liberal majority: it included the ministers of the Linden Grove and Avondale Road chapels, and was chaired by an active Liberal politician. But it also included Dr Warburton, the vicar of the parish in which, at this stage, the school was situated. Later both Mr and Mrs Swithinbank became managers, and they also sat on the committee for the evening continuation (or adult education) school when it opened in Adys Road. Swithinbank referred to the Bellenden Road school as 'extra-parochial', because of its non-denominational teaching, but it was too locally important, and impinged on his own interests and responsibilities too closely, for him to be able to ignore it.[4]

It was, in the first place, a very good school of its kind. Led by an unusually stable senior staff, it built up a reputation in particular for good order and discipline, and for its varied and successful extra-curricular activities. It was well supported from the start, and by 1882 was being warned not to exceed its capacity of twelve hundred pupils. Its significance as a local institution was demonstrated when over seven hundred ex-pupils attended its jubilee celebration in 1898, leading to the formation of an active old scholars' association.[5]

Secondly, the school appears to have been popular with many of Swithinbank's lower middle-class parishioners. When it had first been proposed in 1875 Warburton thought that the inhabitants of the new houses would not be 'likely to send their children to public elementary schools'; but the South London Press proved to be nearer the mark when it spoke of the number of local children likely to be 'in circumstances sufficiently humble to bring them within the School Board range – that of being unable to pay the fees in middle-class schools'.[6] For parents on the Peckham Rye estate in particular the Bellenden Road school was nearer than the National schools attached to All Saints' and St John's. And it was cheaper. Before 1891 the usual cost of a National school was sixpence a week, and that of a Board school three pence[7]: after that date public elementary education was free. The local private dame schools presumably cost more than either of these, and generally offered a genteel rather than a useful education.

When the Bellenden Road school first opened it probably had as many pupils from the streets to the east as from the streets to the west. But after

1880, and especially after the opening of another Board school in Choumert Road, one suspects that the majority came from St Saviour's parish.[8] As we have seen, there was a close link between the Bellenden Road school and St Saviour's Sunday school. The younger Sunday school pupils were in fact taught at the Board school, an institution with which many must have had a week-day familiarity. Swithinbank remarked that his congregation was 'exceptionally rich in Board school teachers', and some of them doubled as teachers in the Sunday school. The school may have helped to soften the divisions between the classes as it did between the religious denominations. The teachers mingled with the parents at events such as the annual school concert, and it may have done lower middle-class children no harm to mix with somewhat rougher pupils from the streets east of Bellenden Road.

Another advantage of the school, from the point of view of socially aspiring parents, was its ability to get pupils into the endowed middle-class secondary schools of the district. In the 1870s there had been very few such schools in south London, St Mary's College in Hanover Park, Peckham being the only local one.[9] But opportunities increased in the 1880s. Mary Datchelor School in Camberwell began to provide a 'liberal and useful education' for 'the daughters of the Middle Class', and for the boys there was Wilson's Grammar School, also in Camberwell, which, as was remarked at the time, looked from the outside remarkably like a Board school. One of Haslam's last engagements was at the Mary Datchelor prize giving in July 1904, when he praised the old girls' society for providing encouragement at 'some of the most difficult and anxious periods' of its members' lives.[10] For the lower middle-class boys of East Dulwich there was Alleyn's School, the 'Lower School' of Dulwich College, which acquired its own buildings in 1887. The achievement of a scholarship to one of these schools, though worth only a few pounds a year, could open social as well as scholastic doors.

1. Jubilee booklet, 1931. In 1884 the distribution of prizes to local Board school children took place at the schoolroom of the Avondale Road chapel. Carter, the Unitarian minister and Correspondent for the Bellenden Road school, was the host, and Gauntlett proposed the vote of thanks. (*SLP*, 15 Nov 1884.)

2. *Magazine*, Jan 1892, Mar 1904.

3. *SLP*, 16 Sept 1905.

4. At an open-air meeting in the playground in July 1898, to celebrate twenty-one years' service by the headmaster, the Church of England, Wesleyans and Baptists all provided lamps to illuminate the proceedings. Carter and Swithinbank were both present. (*SLP*, 14 May 1898.)

5. Southwark Local History Library, notes on Bellenden school records produced for the centenary in 1977.

6. *SLP*, 6 Mar and 13 Nov 1875. The opening of the Bellenden Road school did cause a temporary dip in the numbers of pupils at the National school run by St John's in North Cross Road, but they soon recovered.

7. Even threepence was too much for really poor families (*SLP*, 24 Aug 1878).

8. No register for the school survives for this period. At the end of our period, it should be noted, Grove Vale school became accessible from parts of the parish, through the opening up of roads through the Grove Vale estate.

9. *SLP*, 5 June 1877, 26 July 1878. Although a Church of England foundation, St Mary's was also attended by nonconformist pupils.

10. *Ibid*, 27 Aug 1904.

13.
POOR PEOPLE

IT IS SAID that Bishop King used to look over the city of Lincoln from his palace window and exclaim 'My poor people!'[1] Compassion was a major element in Victorian churchmanship, even if some of the ways in which it was expressed would now be considered patronising. It was thought to be a good thing for a parish to have an area of social deprivation on which to exercise its benevolence[2]; and if it lacked such an area it could, with the agreement of the local clergy concerned, adopt a poor parish some distance away. The nonconformists were also active in what would now be called the voluntary sector. In 1873 the Baptists opened a chapel in Lordship Lane. Those present at the inauguration were told that 'a chapel had two uses, an internal and external one.... The internal life was the worship carried on within its walls.... The external life was the influence which the chapel had upon the surrounding neighbourhood, and the result of that life was seen in the care which was extended to the sick and suffering poor within reach.'[3] When considering, therefore, the 'connectedness' of a church or chapel with its 'surrounding neighbourhood' it is necessary to look at its charitable outreach work, and also to examine what area was thought to be 'within reach'.

Health and sickness were frequently on the minds of the parishioners of St Saviour's. Epidemics, for instance, of smallpox could sweep through the Board school, affecting teachers as well as children. In August 1896 four children died of diphtheria at a house in Choumert Road. The parish was, however, neither large enough nor rich enough to become heavily involved in medical provision. It did not usually support a parish nurse, although for five guineas a year it could call on the services of the Camberwell District Nursing Association, and later it seems to have been associated with a similar organisation in Peckham.[4] The vicar kept a small fund, about £25, for use in emergencies when short-term nursing was required.[5] Another way in which the church could help was in providing 'hospital letters' – letters of recommendation to a particular charitable institution. The vicar was the key person here, but much depended on the efficient reporting of cases by the parish visitors. In November 1903 we find Haslam, bereft of this necessary help, wasting time in 'fruitless searches for persons enquired after by correspondents, or in need of hospital or some other help.'

In January 1896 Swithinbank wrote that the parochial 'stream of benevolence' was directed mainly towards 'the great organised charities of South London, especially those that are medical, such as Guy's and St Thomas's, and the Camberwell Provident Dispensary.' It was to such institutions that the proceeds of Hospital Sunday were sent, and in an average year as much as £75, half the parish's total charitable giving, went to hospitals. Guy's and St Thomas's were reasonably accessible by public transport, and before the move of King's College Hospital to Denmark Hill were Peckham's nearest major hospitals. (The infirmaries of Camberwell and East Dulwich were Poor Law places, to be avoided by respectable people if possible.) Giving money to hospitals was not entirely altruistic. Swithinbank himself had two spells in Guy's, the second, when he was feeling the financial pinch, in a public ward.

Among more specialist hospitals the parish had a particularly strong link with the Evelina Hospital for Sick Children in Southwark. The idea of supporting it came from the Sunday school. Every year thirty pounds was raised to fund a cot, and each month a middle-class lady, not necessarily directly connected with St Saviour's, would visit the occupant and supply a report to the parish magazine. The Evelina, now part of St Thomas's, had been established in a poor district for 'children of the poor only', but Camberwell and Peckham fell within its catchment area, and in 1892 one of the occupants of the sponsored cot was a St Saviour's Sunday school pupil herself.

Following a spell in hospital a period of convalescence, perhaps in the purer air of a seaside resort, might be prescribed. This could be costly. The vicar had another small pot of money earmarked for convalescent expenses, but as with hospitals the most practical form of help could come in the form of a letter of recommendation. The Yarrow Home at Broadstairs was one of those places deemed suitable for convalescent children. Its low charges catered for parents who were 'under the obligation of maintaining a respectable appearance on very restricted means', including ministers on small stipends, widows who had seen better days, unsuccessful professional men, clerks with small salaries and skilled foremen. The children themselves did not have to be Anglican, but their home training was expected to 'render them fit companions for other respectable and well-mannered children'. One can see why the Yarrow Home thought it worthwhile to advertise in St Saviour's magazine.[6]

* * * * *

Illness could result in acute financial hardship where families existed on small margins, and so could losing one's job. The mid 1880s and the early 1890s were times of winter unemployment and widespread distress in London. (An employment register was being kept at the verger's house in January 1892.) But in a parish like St Saviour's periods of family crisis could be concealed behind the lace curtains, a phenomenon referred to by the curate Alan Gordon Smith (he of the Champion Hill Browning Circle) in a revealing piece for the Magazine for January 1892.

> Persons who come down the hill to our Church can have little idea of the actual condition of some families even in the tidy-looking houses which they pass, and may hardly be aware that our parish runs, though not deeply, into the poorer districts of East Dulwich and Peckham. Every year our streets become less 'well-to-do', more houses become sub-let, three and even four families being found under one roof, and people who two years ago were in a position to help others are now compelled to accept relief themselves.

> There has always been more poverty amongst us than appears on the surface: often it is the poverty of those who have looked on better days, to whom a mere dole is worse than useless.

Swithinbank was away from the parish when this was published, but he reprinted it in subsequent numbers of the Magazine, appending a summary of the parish's activities in this area. In addition to the Evelina Cot and the hospital letters he noted the stock of good white blankets issued in November for return in the spring, three well-stocked maternity boxes available from the Vicarage, a provident club managed by 'ladies of the congregation', a library for the sick (in course of assembly), the distribution of items given at the harvest festival or made by the girls' sewing club, and a small private fund kept by the vicar mainly to assist 'I poveri vergognosi' (the strayed and fallen). We are told that relief was not confined to the Anglican poor, although 'now and then by giving, or redeeming from pawn, a coat or dress, we enable parents to attend Church', or their offspring to go to Sunday school.[7]

The occupants of some of the 'tidy-looking houses' may not have thought much of Gordon Smith's piece; and we have seen how some of the Sunday school parents could resent any perceived implication that their children were not well-behaved enough to go on the annual treat.[8] When it came to the handling of individual cases, however, the parochial authorities appreciated the need to tread carefully. In January 1890 Magazine readers were told that the vicar and Miss Headon of Grove Park (presumably a visitor) had the details of the case of the 'W family', but that 'consideration for the family forbids the papers being scattered broadcast'.

Although Gordon Smith's article referred only to the parish, it is likely that its social work occasionally extended a little way over the boundary in the Bellenden Road area. In July 1896 one of the visiting districts was called the 'outside district'. The parish also supported a creche at 64 Choumert Road (in All Saints' parish), founded in 1898 to 'take charge of the little children of poor mothers, who are, in some cases, the sole breadwinners of the family'. It charged threepence a day for nursing and toddler-minding, and kept a register for women seeking work. Mrs Carrington and another lady represented St Saviour's on the committee.[9] Farther afield there was no direct link, at least in Swithinbank's time, with any one poor London parish. When he came to St Saviour's he had in fact found such a link, with St Mary's, Haggerston, but had terminated it in favour of more local help for the poor of St Saviour's and St John's. Thereafter the parish confined itself to responding to particular appeals, such as the Lord Mayor's Mansion House Fund. Money from the offertory was sent to St Luke's Deptford and St George's Camberwell in January 1888; and in July 1904 there was a garden party at Church House for 'poor crippled children from the slums of Bermondsey'.[10]

Swithinbank was conscious of the need to take advice on matters of charity 'wisdom', and did so from the Camberwell Provident Dispensary, the Dulwich Council for the Relief of Distress and the Dulwich branch of the Charity Organisation Society (the last-named, with its emphasis on helping only the deserving poor, a cause close to the heart of Francis Peek).[11] But such bodies were looking old-fashioned by the end of the century. More modern-sounding were the free legal advice centres at Cambridge House and Browning Hall, in Camberwell and Walworth respectively. A vicar's letter might still be useful for those intending to use them, but it was not required.[12]

1. Told to me when staying in Diocesan House (the Old Palace), Lincoln in 1966.
2. Cox, *The English Churches in a Secular Society*, p30, quoting a south London incumbent.
3. *SLP*, 4 Jan 1873.
4. *Magazine*, Oct 1892, May 1898, June 1903, June 1904.
5. *Ibid*, June 1905.
6. *Ibid*, Apr 1897, June 1898. The writer and poet Richard Church, the south London son of a clerk and a Board school teacher, describes a spell in the Yarrow Home in *Over the Bridge* (1956 repr, pp174ff).
7. A pawn shop had appeared in Bellenden Road by 1891.
8. For the Sunday school row of 1885 see above, chapter 4.
9. *Magazine*, Apr and Dec 1898, July 1905.
10. *Ibid*, Aug 1884, July 1904; *SLP*, 7 Jan 1888.
11. *Magazine*, May 1898.
12. *Ibid*, Aug 1898.

14.
LIFE AND LEISURE IN SOUTH LONDON

THE NEW SUBURBS that sprang up in south London in the 1870s could lack a clear local context. Occupying what had previously been fields or market gardens, they lay sometimes in a kind of no-man's land between the older settlements, and it could be difficult to know what to call them. Some developments were called New This or New That, whilst others were named to emphasise their nearness to a railway station. To add to their topographical ambivalence, they fitted uneasily into existing administrative structures. Much of south London still formed part of the county of Surrey and, until 1877, the diocese of Winchester. The Peckham Rye and Denmark Park estates found themselves in the parliamentary borough of Lambeth, a product of the 1832 Reform Act that did not make much local sense. For civil purposes they were in the parish of Camberwell, whose vestry in the 1870s was struggling to keep up with the rapid influx of population. In January 1878 a resident of Avondale Road, indignant at the poor state of the local streets, complained that the vestry 'took no more notice of us than if we lived in the backwoods of America'.[1]

Gradually institutions were adapted or reformed to meet the new demands on them. The new diocese of Rochester, as we have seen, was among the less successful responses to the challenges of the period. The 1885 redistribution of parliamentary seats, however, produced a new constituency of Dulwich with which local voters could more easily identify. Some of the candidates were well-known local personalities, such as James Henderson, the proprietor of the *South London Press*, and Edwin Jones, a founding partner in the Rye Lane department store of Jones and Higgins. In 1900 the parish of Camberwell was upgraded to borough status, and the accompanying creation of smaller wards led to a renewed interest in local politics by residents such as Edwin Gauntlett, who stood successfully for the Lyndhurst ward.[2] By 1905, indeed, there were numerous opportunities for involvement in local affairs. One could stand for, or at least vote for representatives on, the Board of Guardians, the School Board for London, and, from 1889, the London County Council as well as the borough.

It was a somewhat similar story with the clubs, societies and other organisations that helped to cement local society. Already by the early 1870s there were a number of bodies that covered south London as a whole, but they tended to be rather specialist, being devoted to such subjects as photography or microscopy, and one suspects that they were middle-class affairs. More local clubs and societies were to be found in the older village centres of Camberwell, Peckham and Dulwich, but they may not have been very welcoming to suburban newcomers.[3] In the early days of the Peckham Rye estate the Victoria Tavern, though just off the estate itself at the southern end of Victoria Road, was the nearest centre of social life. It had a flourishing cricket club, that numbered the builder Edward Terry among its members, and at the general election of 1880 it provided a committee room for the local Conservatives.[4] But not everybody sought the beery conviviality of a public house.[5]

Not surprisingly the churches and chapels were ready to fill the gap, and for the parish of St Saviour's the church and the two chapels were undoubtedly important in consolidating the social fabric of the new suburb. Thereafter they became relatively less prominent, as the range of clubs and societies available locally grew, and as the places where such bodies could meet also multiplied. Cricket clubs, horticultural societies and choral societies seem to have been among the earlier bodies to be formed locally, but later on there was a growth in other cultural activities, particularly literary and debating; and cricket clubs were supplemented by clubs devoted to cycling, tennis, swimming, athletics and, especially towards the end of the century, football. In the immediate neighbourhood the Victoria Tavern was joined by the Ivanhoe Hotel in 1880 and the Oglander in 1883: by the early 1890s they both had literary and other societies attached to them. Other local institutions and businesses developed their own social life. Jones and Higgins, for instance, a large local employer, had a glee club, and the Liberal and Conservative associations that sprang up in the 1880s diversified into social activities. Young men played billiards while waiting for the next election, rather as Drake had played bowls while awaiting the Spanish Armada.[6]

A further development was the increasing availability of public halls, which could provide either public entertainments or places for meetings of a more private kind. In the early 1880s one could hire the local public baths, skating rink or Masonic hall, but by 1905 there were public halls in Rye Lane, Shawbury Road (off Lordship Lane) and Grove Vale. The Imperial Hall in Grove Vale was built in 1902 to meet a demand from local people who 'did not want to go far afield for their entertainment and amusement'. It was intended to cater for 'all kinds of people', and could be hired for receptions, suppers, dances and smoking concerts.[7] For those who *were* prepared to go farther afield the trams that passed the Imperial Hall could take them to Camberwell and beyond for the delights of the south London theatres and music halls. For others there were by 1905 museums and art galleries also within easy reach, not to mention that great south London draw the Crystal Palace.

Lower middle-class women would not normally go inside a pub, and we are told that they disliked smoking concerts[8], but by 1905 the range of social activities available to women in south London had grown enormously. Ladies played tennis, rode bicycles and did gymnastic exercises. The serious-minded could join the Women's Liberal Association, or even become Poor Law guardians. Rye Lane was a Mecca for shopping, and by the end of our period the *South London Press* was running a weekly column for women, although it tended to concentrate on topics such as shopping and fashion.

Compared with the 1870s, however, the local paper carried fewer reports of church and chapel events. Changing social habits were undoubtedly having their effect on religious life. An increased emphasis on leisure activities did not just mean the opportunity to go to a music hall rather than an improving church-related gathering: it also introduced the temptation of going to Peckham Rye or Dulwich Park, or taking one's bicycle into the country, instead of attending a Sunday service. The annual holiday, a growing habit among the somewhat better-off, had its impact at St Saviour's. The Easter break reduced attendances at that festival, and hence the amount of the Easter offering; whilst by 1903 Haslam could refer to a 'general exodus' in August, although conscientious activists might interrupt their own holidays in order to organise a parish treat.[9] In August 1896 Swithinbank had suggested to readers of the Magazine that they could set aside five shillings from their holiday money and give it to church funds: this would after all mean for the men only 'a dozen cigars less or going without a game of billiards and drinks, for the women two mornings on the beach instead of evenings on the pier.'

Many south London priests worried about declining church attendances. And we have seen that the numbers at St Saviour's did indeed fall over the period. It is also true that secularism was making advances locally. There were Sunday morning debates, for instance, on Peckham Rye Common, although such meetings were not allowed in the parks.[10] But it may be suggested that the average lower middle-class family in St Saviour's parish was not becoming noticeably less religious, even if its attendance at Sunday worship was becoming less regular. Probably not many young clerks were being converted to radical socialism, and not many young ladies were losing their faith through reading secularist books borrowed from the public library.[11]

1. *SLP*, 19 Jan 1878. A protest meeting was held at the Unitarian chapel.

2. *Ibid*, 27 Oct 1900, 7 Nov 1903.

3. *Ibid*, 2 Feb and 23 Mar 1878.

4. *Ibid*, 12 Oct 1878.

5. In 1879 the Clapham Junction area was reported to be 'badly off for a place where the respectable middle class can spend an evening without resorting to the so-called hotels of the neighbourhood …. There are a large number of bankers' clerks and persons engaged in the Civil Service and in mercantile houses in the City who would gladly avail themselves of such a club.' (*SLP*, 12 July 1879.)

6. *Ibid*, 2 Feb 1884.

7. *Ibid*, 1 Feb 1902.

8. *Ibid*, 9 Nov 1905.

9. But not all the families connected with St Saviour's had an annual seaside holiday. Of 190 Sunday school pupils who joined a trip to Herne Bay in 1905, forty were seeing the sea for the first time. (*Magazine*, Aug 1905.) Railway excursions for Sunday school children were commonplace by this date.

10. *SLP*, 1 Feb 1902. For Lambeth see Cox, *English Churches in a Secular Society*, pp37, 182, 198-9 *et passim*. For more general anxieties about the spread of secularism and disrespect for the Sabbath see Cox, *op cit*, pp22-3 and McLeod, *Class and Religion*, pp224-32.

11. For the debate on whether industrialisation and urbanisation were responsible for the late Victorian decline in religious belief see for instance Green, *Religion in the Age of Decline*, pp2-20. More recent work has argued against any straightforward link between the two; and in any case the collapse of 'Christian culture' is now located in the 1960s rather than the late nineteenth century (see Callum G Brown, *The Death of Christian Britain: understanding secularisation 1800-2000*, 2001; Hugh McLeod, *The Religious Crisis of the 1960s*, 2007).

15.
CONCLUDING REMARKS

IN DECEMBER 1874 a new church was opened at the southern end of Lordship Lane. St Peter's, Dulwich Common was to serve a growing suburb in the south of the older parish of St John's, much of it on land developed by the British Land Company. As the *South London Press* pointed out, the area was a pleasant one, but 'without that distinctive character which is so important in promoting a feeling of unity among the inhabitants.' St Peter's would help to rectify this: it 'will do much to remove this disjointed state of things', and 'will complete and localise what has hitherto been unfinished and straggling.'[1]

Unfinished and straggling the suburb certainly was. It was being developed slowly and somewhat haphazardly, and with no provision for public buildings or amenities. This left the field open for voluntary organisations to assist the process of building a local community, and the Church's contribution was what might be called a 'landmark' place of worship. It was erected on a prominent site, given by the Dulwich College estate, and a few years later it was completed by a steeple, the gift of the tea merchant Frederick Horniman, that provided a focal point for the neighbourhood.

The development of the Peckham Rye and Denmark Park estates followed a different course. The British Land Company made no concession to community needs, any more than it had done on its East Dulwich estate, but the suburb was smaller and much more compact, with relatively clear boundaries, and was nearly complete by 1881. Perhaps therefore it had less need of a landmark church. It did not get one. Haslam later lamented that St Saviour's had been 'built in an out-of-the-way and blind street, without any spire or manifestation of its presence'. Even the bell that was meant to ring out over the neighbourhood, summoning the faithful to prayer, was poor and unmusical.[2] As far as landmarks went, the most prominent building in the parish was the Board school, and the Free Methodists had been quicker off the mark than the Anglicans, acquiring the best corner site on the Peckham Rye estate for their chapel. St Saviour's, then, was unlikely to dominate its neighbourhood, but it stood a good chance of attracting a loyal congregation from the surrounding streets, and of fostering a sense of belonging at least among its committed adherents.

Stephenson got the parish off to a good start. He was young and enthusiastic, and so, one imagines, was the majority of his congregation. Couples flocked to his services, and in due course brought their infants to the font and sent their children to the rapidly-growing Sunday school. He seems to have understood the importance of 'community', even if he did not use the word: witness his encouragement of secular activities such as the cricket club. But after this short initial period, which ended with Stephenson's own early death, the progress of the parish was not so smooth. The next incumbent, Herbert Swithinbank, was a High Churchman, and during his ministry there was a tendency to concentrate on the worship of the church to the detriment of the social side of parish life. His successor, John Haslam, attempted to readjust these priorities, but all too soon he ran into difficulties, and when he died in 1904 it was necessary for the next incumbent to take the parish somewhat firmly in hand.

It is a mistake, however, to overestimate the power of the clergy to shape the life of a parish. They could arrange weekday services, for instance, but fail to get more than two or three people to attend them; they could set up parochial organisations but could not ensure their popularity; and unless they were of independent means they could not avoid a certain degree of dependence on the wealthier members of their congregations. In fact St Saviour's developed its own parochial character during the period 1881-1905 without being too disturbed by changes of incumbent. Traditions, once established, were maintained, and major upheavals and schisms avoided. The church continued to be known for its well-presented services and its well-organised Sunday school, but in other respects there were persistent deficiencies. Youth work was a perennial weakness; and clubs and societies connected with the church often withered before they had had a chance to take root. Nor was St Saviour's remarkable for its outreach work. Missions, in the evangelical sense, were not a prominent feature. And charitable activity was limited: it tended to end, as it began, at home. In other words, there were problems with both bonding and bridging.[3] Were there any underlying local or social factors to which these characteristics of parish life can be attributed?

To start with, it is difficult to attach any great significance to the shape of the parish and the way in which the boundaries had been drawn. This is largely because so little attention was paid to them. Even if they had some importance, for some people, in the early days, twenty-five years later they were being largely ignored. It was a situation that the clergy recognised, and indeed to which they themselves contributed. In places the boundaries followed physical barriers, but elsewhere those who crossed them were probably not even aware that they were doing so. On the other hand the topography of the *suburb*, as distinct from the parish, may well have had an effect on local attitudes. It began as something of an enclave, and managed to preserve its identity over the following twenty-five years. It was never subject to incursions of people displaced from other districts, and never threatened with undesirable commercial or industrial developments. No busy tram route was engineered through the estates, and the local streets remained quiet during the day. In such a sheltered neighbourhood the plight of the destitute in Southwark or Bermondsey would have seemed remote, and the mission fields of Africa or India a world away.

If the parish boundaries turn out to have had a minimal effect on the character of the parish, other aspects of the way in which it was set up in 1881 were definitely more influential. Like many other parishes St Saviour's had a higher end and a lower end, and as was frequently the case the folk at, and just beyond, the top end were socially as well as topographically superior to those farther down. The Church of England was good at reminding the rich of their duty to the poor, but it was also rather good at emphasising the gulf between the two. Even at the heart of parish life, the Sunday services, distinctions of place were linked to distinctions of class. The seat-rent system separated the regular core of worshippers from the casual periphery, with the poorer members of the congregation tending to occupy the free seats. Gender was another divisive factor, although less in evidence by the early twentieth century.

Even more fundamental to the social character of the parish, however, was the dominant influence within it of the lower middle class. It was that section of society that set the tone not only of the suburb but, increasingly as the years went on, of the church itself. It included the clerks, civil servants, school teachers and others who, as we saw in chapter seven, did much of the day-to-day work of the parish. The clergy, impeccably middle- (as opposed to lower middle-) class themselves, may not always have felt comfortable in this cultural environment, but they had to live with it.

It is easy to be rude about the Victorian lower middle class – though hard to be quite as rude as Matthew Arnold, when he epitomised it as 'so drugged with business' that its senses were blunt to any stimulus except religion. Even that religion, he averred, was 'narrow, unintelligent, repulsive'.[4] This comes close to caricature, or at least to stereotype. For a start, not all lower middle-class people were conservative churchmen. And those who attended St Saviour's included a good few who, according to their lights, worked hard for their neighbours and fellow-worshippers. Nevertheless it is possible to see how some of the characteristic features of parish life corresponded with the *mores* of the lower middle class.

The bright and attractive Sunday services, for instance, had a particular appeal for those whose weekday world, whether at the office or at home, lacked colour, variety and stimulus. The family atmosphere of St Saviour's had a strong resonance, and the appearance of the family at church, arrayed in its Sunday best, was a clear indication of respectability. The white-collar worker understood the 'importance of dress' well enough: if he turned up for work looking down-at-heel he stood to lose his job.[5] During the week, on the other hand, the white-collar family had little time for organised religion. Even the committed church workers of Copleston Road do not seem to have supported the weekday services. It was partly the act of going to church that made Sunday *different* from other days.

CONCLUDING REMARKS

Apart, again, from the committed church workers, the lower middle-class parishioners of St Saviour's do not seem to have been good at 'bonding'. Suburbia has been described as 'a collective effort to lead a private life',[6] and the very lay-out of the streets and houses encouraged people to keep themselves to themselves. When the inhabitants of these houses went to church they tended to keep a low profile. They liked a well-presented service in a clean, warm and comfortable church, but they were not always keen to help pay for these benefits. If they were dissatisfied they would not voice their views openly, but the vicar might become aware from time to time of grumbling in private. By the time Daukes came to the parish it had acquired the reputation of being 'difficult'.[7] This may at first sight seem a strange description, but I suspect that it was to these back-bench attitudes that he was referring. And as with bonding, so with bridging. Especially towards the end of the century, the average salary earner was having to work too hard to keep his own family to have much time or money to spare for charitable or outreach work. Horizons could undoubtedly be very narrow.

Lower middle-class people sometimes preferred to move on rather than put down roots in a particular suburb; but that did not mean that they had no sense of locality. They were well aware of the differences, visually and socially, between one part of suburbia and another. They could tell if one side or end of a street was 'better' than another, and they could detect the change in environment that one might experience, for instance, in crossing under or over a railway line, such as the one that all but separated the Peckham Rye from the Denmark Park estate.[8] But whereas middle-class patrons and working-class clients of the parish church might have their reasons for knowing where the *parish* boundaries lay, these reasons did not apply to lower middle-class parishioners (except perhaps when it came to getting married). As we saw in chapter nine, they did not think it disloyal to 'shop around' for a local church that suited their tastes and requirements, provided as a rule that it was within reasonable walking distance.

* * * * *

In 1931, when St Saviour's celebrated its jubilee, both church and parish would still have seemed familiar to those who had lived and worshipped there in the 1880s. But the following fifty years saw major social and religious changes. Socially the first change, already under way in 1931, was the demise of the Grove Hill and Champion Hill area as a select middle-class suburb. Many of the large old villas came down, and were replaced by much larger blocks of Council flats. St Saviour's not only lost its few remaining wealthy supporters but found itself with greatly enlarged boundaries: the area and population of the parish were doubled, and most of the new parishioners were Council tenants. More devastating, however, were the effects of the Second World War. The church itself and the vicarage were damaged, and so were many private houses, some beyond repair. Old residents moved out, and evacuees from poorer and worse-damaged areas of inner London moved in, significantly changing the social composition of the suburb. Its respectable lower middle-class character gave way to a more disparate and less class-ridden local society.

In religious terms the Church, here and elsewhere in south London, had to come to terms with the growing secularism of post-War society. St Saviour's may have benefited to a small extent from the 'mini-revival' that Church historians have identified in the 1950s, but by the mid-1960s the church was shabby and in need of repair, the congregation shrinking and the parish generally in low water. It was during this decade, nevertheless, that a new start was made. A movement towards ecumenical worship and greater outreach culminated in the late 1970s in the coming together of St Saviour's with Hanover Chapel, the United Reformed church that had since 1920 occupied the former Free Methodist chapel in Bellenden Road, and the creation of a new community centre in part of the church building.[9]

By 1981, the church's centenary year, it was clear that an old world had given place to a new. Gone were the traditional church interior and the elaborate services cherished and enjoyed by earlier generations. Gone too were the crowded Sunday school and other features of Victorian and post-Victorian parish life. In their place was an innovative project more relevant to the realities of south London society in the late twentieth century.

1. *SLP*, 10 Oct 1874. The article was doubtless written by the newspaper's owner, James Henderson, who lived locally at Adon Mount.

2. *Magazine*, Sept 1901.

3. For bonding and bridging see above, chapter 8. These two types of activity are not completely different from one another. Indeed it could be said that without good bonding it is difficult to have successful bridging.

4. Quoted in Gillian Tindall, *The Fields Beneath*, p157. For the stultifying nature of suburban life see also Sir Walter Besant, *London in the Nineteenth Century*, pp262-3, quoted in Donald J Olsen, *The Growth of Victorian London*, London 1975, pp213-14. Both Arnold and Besant, it must be said, refer to the middle, rather than specifically the lower middle, class.

5. John R Kellett, *The Impact of Railways on Victorian Cities*, London 1969, p380.

6. Lewis Mumford, quoted in Putnam, *Bowling Alone*, p210.

7. Daukes used the word at a meeting at Church House shortly after his induction (*SLP*, 11 Feb 1905). In September 1902 Haslam had written that 'many use the Church and criticise it, but do little or nothing towards its support.'

8. For the 'district consciousness' of the lower middle class see McLeod, *Class and Religion*, pp11-12, and 'White Collar Values and the role of Religion' in Geoffrey Crossick, ed, *The Lower Middle Class in Britain 1870-1914*, p70. For railway lines as barriers between one district and another see, eg, Gillian Tindall, *The Fields Beneath*, p168.

9. See *The Copleston Story, a celebration of the Copleston Centre 1978-2001*, pr 2001. The scheme was financed by the sales of Hanover Chapel and Church House. The Institute had been sold in 1969.

PRINCIPAL SOURCES

A. ARCHIVES

(i) *The National Archives*

RG 10/723, 730; RG 11/674, 676; RG 12/465-6; RG 13/498 census enumerators' returns 1871, 1881, 1891, 1901. (Microfilm and fiche copies in Southwark Local History Library.)

C 104/173 deeds for McDermott's estates (Chancery Masters' Exhibits, McDermott *v* Kealy).

(ii) *British Library*

Files of the South London Press 1870-1905 and other local (south London) newspapers. (Microfilm copies in Southwark Local History Library.)

(iii) *Lambeth Palace Library*

Papers of Archbishop Tait, vol 285.

ECE/7/1/59883 Church Commissioners' files (temporarily deposited by the Church of England Record Centre): St Saviour's Champion Hill 1879-1947.

ECE/7/1/47447, ECE/7/112140, CC/7/1/CB/796, 1038 *Ibid*: St John the Evangelist East Dulwich.

ECE/7/1/35240 *Ibid*: All Saints' Blenheim Grove.

(iv) *Guildhall Library, London*

MS 31633 Peek, Winch and Co, private ledger 1855-78.

(v) *London Metropolitan Archives*: *parish records of St Saviour's Denmark Park*

A/01, 02 registers of baptisms and marriages.

A/04/1-2 Confirmation registers 1887-94 (with roll of communicants 1888-1900 and summaries of Easter communicants 1881-5, 1893-4, 1896), 1902-68.

PRINCIPAL SOURCES

B/01/001-003 service registers 1881-92.
B/02/001 miscellaneous papers, including extract from the *London Gazette* 1881, orders of service (inductions of Swithinbank, Haslam and Daukes) and copy of licence for lay readers.
D/01/002 ground plan of church 1881.
G/01-2 vestry book 1881-1913; church council and PCC minutes 1908-28.
J/01/001-006 parish magazines 1890-92, June 1893, 1896-1905.

(vi) *London Metropolitan Archives: Rochester diocesan records*
DR/CP/30 consecration papers, St Saviour's Denmark Park 1881.
DR/OP/49 parsonage papers, the same 1879-82.

(vii) *London Metropolitan Archives: other records*
Microfilmed registers of baptisms for St John the Evangelist East Dulwich, St Giles's Camberwell and Camden Chapel Peckham.
MBW/1687/41, MBW/1789 Metropolitan Board of Works, Camberwell district surveyor's returns 1879 and drainage applications 1872-4.
LCC/EO/PS/12/B30/1-48 inspectors' reports, Bellenden Road School 1879-1959.
Acc 2831/1 St Saviour's Sunday school, teachers' minute book 1886-94.

(viii) *Southwark Local History Library*
Civil parish of Camberwell: rate book 1859; valuation lists 1870, 1900 (no 3687); vestry minutes (GPC) 1872-3 (3/251).
1984/256; roll 60 abstract of title, Peckham Rye estate 1873, with map of plots for auction 13 Oct 1873.
Papers relating to Bellenden Road school *c*1977, including notes from a log book the original of which was subsequently lost.

(ix) *Minet Library, Lambeth*
12006-12 McDermott deeds (BRA 898).
Extra-illustrated copy of WH Blanch's History of Camberwell (1875), with additions by WF Noble.

(x) *Lewisham Local Studies Library*
A 64/1 Mayow Adams deeds and papers (BRA 1272), including McDermott deeds.
NM 1/1/3/1 Sydenham and Forest Hill Methodist Circuit records: UMFC circuit minute book 1908-26.

(xi) *St Saviour's Denmark Park: records in parish custody*
Parish magazines 1883, 1884 (2 vols).
Printed map of the parish *c*1890.
Miscellaneous photographs.
Miscellaneous printed items, including cricket club rules and fixture list 1883 (1 item) and copy of Jubilee booklet 1931.
Copy of *Sermons by the late Rev JJ Stephenson, Vicar of St Saviour's Denmark Park, with an introductory preface by the Lord Bishop of Rochester,* London 1884.

(xii) *St John the Evangelist East Dulwich: records in parish custody*
Parish magazines 1885-6.
Vestry book 1880s.

(xiii) *All Saints Blenheim Grove: records in parish custody*
Baptismal registers 1867-1905 (4 vols).

B. PRINTED BOOKS

John D Beasley, *Peckham and Nunhead Churches*, [1995].
DW Bebbington, *Evangelicalism in Modern Britain: a history from the 1730s to the 1980s*, London 1989.
Sir Walter Besant, *London South of the Thames*, 1912 edn.
Mary Boast, *St John's, East Dulwich: Church and Parish*, 1991.
Charles Booth, *Labour and the Life of the People*, Vol II, Appendix, 1891; *Streets and Population Classified*, 1892, with map 1889.
Chris Brooks and Andrew Saint, eds, *The Victorian Church: architecture and society*, Manchester 1995.
[WS Clarke], *The Suburban Homes of London: a residential guide*, London 1881.
Jeffrey Cox, *The English Churches in a Secular Society: Lambeth 1870-1930*, New York and Oxford 1982.
Geoffrey Crossick, ed, *The Lower Middle Classes in Britain 1870-1914*, London 1977.
MJ Daunton, *House and Home in the Victorian City: working-class housing 1850-1914*, London 1983.
HJ Dyos, *Victorian Suburb: a study of the growth of Camberwell*, Leicester 1959, repr 1973.

Revd TJ Gaster, *A Brief History of the Parish of All Saints, Camberwell*, [*c*1897] (incomplete photocopy in Southwark Local History Library).

SJD Green, *Religion in the Age of Decline: organisation and experience in industrial Yorkshire 1870-1920,* Cambridge 1996.

WJA Hahn, ed, *A History of the Parish of St John the Evangelist, East Dulwich 1865-1951,* [1951].

Alan Haig, *The Victorian Clergy*, London 1984.

Mrs Jas A Heaton, *Origins of the Diocese of Southwark 1877-1905*, Southampton 1950.

John R Kellett, *The Impact of Railways on Victorian Cities*, London 1969.

Frances Knight, *The Nineteenth-century Church and English Society*, Cambridge 1995.

David McIlhiney, *A Gentleman in Every Slum: Church of England missions in East London 1837—1914*, Pennsylvania 1988.

Hugh McLeod, *Class and Religion in the Victorian City*, London 1974.

– , 'White collar values and the role of religion', in Geoffrey Crossick, *op cit*, pp61-88.

– , ed, *European Religion in the Age of Great Cities 1830-1930*, London and New York 1995.

JN Morris, *Religion and Urban Change: Croydon 1840-1914*, Woodbridge 1992.

Stephen Muthesius, *The English Terraced House*, New Haven and London 1982.

David J Olsen, *The Growth of Victorian London*, London 1976.

Robert D Putnam, *Bowling Alone: the collapse and revival of American community*, New York and London 2000.

Janet Roebuck, *Urban Development in Nineteenth-century London: Lambeth, Battersea and Wandsworth 1838-1888*, London and Chichester 1979.

St Clement's. *History of the Parish Church of St Clement, East Dulwich*, [1932].

St Peter's. *St Peter's Church, Dulwich Common: Jubilee Record 1924*, repr 1966.

Mark Smith, *Religion in Industrial Society: Oldham and Saddleworth 1740-1865*, Oxford 1994.

KDM Snell, *Parish and Belonging: community, identity and welfare in England and Wales 1700-1950*, Cambridge 2006.

– and Paul S Ell, *Rival Jerusalems: the geography of Victorian religion*, Cambridge 2000.

The Streets of London: the Booth notebooks, south-east, London 1997.

FML Thompson, *Hampstead: building a borough 1650-1964*, London and Boston 1974.

Gillian Tindall, *The Fields Beneath: the history of a London village*, London 1977.

HP White, *A Regional History of the Railways of Great Britain: vol III, Greater London*, London 1963.

Sarah Williams, 'Urban popular religion and the Rites of Passage', in Hugh McLeod, ed, *European Religion in the Age of Great Cities*, pp216-36.

Nigel Yates, *Anglican Ritualism in Victorian Britain 1830-1910*, Oxford 1999.

Stephen Yeo, *Religion and Voluntary Organisations in Crisis*, London 1976.

INDEX

All Saints', Blenheim Grove, 27, 29, 34, 63, 69, 83-4, 87, 88, 99
All Saints', South Lambeth, 39
artisans, *see* craftsmen
Avondale Road (now Rise), Peckham Rye, 5, 6, 17, 93, 108
  see also Unitarian chapel
Ayers, Ann or Anna, 2

Bellenden Road, Peckham Rye, 5, 6, 14, 27-9, 78, 80, 93, 94
  see also Free Methodist chapel
Bellenden Road Board School, 47, 55, 72, 94, 96, 98-100, 102
  see also School Board for London
Benington, RC, medical practitioner and churchwarden, 62
boarders, 14, 15
Booth, Charles, social investigator, 15, 19 n7
boundaries, parochial, 27-9, 61, 78-84, 115, 117, 118
Bristowe family, of Camberwell, 56
British Land Company, 3-7, 26, 30, 113
Bromar Road, Denmark Park, 5, 8, 9, 13, 14, 15, 17, 27
Burnham, Walter M, advertising contractor and churchwarden, 61-2

Camberwell, xiv, 95, 103, 109, 110
  civil parish (later borough), 108, 109
  District Nursing Association, 103
  ecclesiastical parish, xiii, xiv, 78; *and see also* St Giles's
  Mary Datchelor School, 100
  Provident Dispensary, 103, 106
  Wilson's Grammar School, 100
  workhouse, 17, 103
Camberwell Grove, 27, 57, 61
Camden Church, Peckham Road, 83
Carolin, J Sinclair, curate of St Saviour's, 39, 42 n21
Carrington, Henry, draper and churchwarden, 49, 63
Carrington, Mrs, 106
Carter, George, Unitarian minister, 94, 101 ns 1, 4
Champion Hill, Camberwell, 3, 7, 17, 29, 57, 75, 118
  Browning Circle, 74
  Station, *see* East Dulwich
Charity Organisation Society, 23, 106
Choumert Road, Peckham Rye, 5, 46, 102, 105-6
Christian, Ewan, Rochester diocesan architect, 26
Church, Richard, writer and poet, 16, 107 n6
Clapham Junction, 112 n5
clerks, xlv, 12, 15, 16, 18, 55, 63, 104, 112 n5, 116
  see also lower middle class
community feeling, xiv, xv, 12, 15, 35, 48, 70-5, 109-10, 113-17
  see also parochial consciousness
commuting, *see* transport
Copleston Road, Peckham Rye, 5-9, 13-18, 25, 27, 34, 57, 62-4, 72-4, 78, 80
  see also St Saviour's, Denmark Park
Couratin family, clerks and church activists, 63-4
craftsmen, 12, 29, 55, 95
cricket clubs, 76 n14, 109
  see also St Saviour's, Denmark Park
Cut-throat Lane, 2, 10 n7, 78
cycling, 80, 110, 111

Dale, AHP, bank manager and churchwarden, 62
Dalston, HM, of Grove Lane, Camberwell, 61
Danby Street, Peckham Rye, 5, 11, 12, 14, 15, 18, 62, 94
Daukes, Francis Whitfield, vicar of St Saviour's, 38-9, 44, 47, 51, 57, 74, 117
Daukes, Samuel Whitfield, vicar of Holy Trinity, New Beckenham, 23, 27, 41 n16
Denmark Hill, 17, 57, 62, 103
   Station, 7
   see also Lava Skating Rink; Lutheran chapel
Denmark Park Estate, 7-9, 11-18, 27, 29, 60, 80, 108
Dulwich, 63, 109
   College, 100, 113
   Park, 111
   see also East Dulwich; St Barnabas's; West Dulwich

East Dulwich, xiii, xiv, 17, 25, 95, 100, 104
   Friern Manor Farm estate, 5
   Poor Law institutions, 17, 103
   Station, 17
   see also Grove Vale; St Clement's; St John the Evangelist; St Peter's, Dulwich Common
Ecclesiastical Commissioners, xii-xiii, 26-7, 30, 78
Eglinton, Arthur, vicar of St John's, 90
Ellyatt, George, builder and churchwarden, 60, 62
Emmanuel Church, West Dulwich, 23

Fabritius, JC, of Barry Road, East Dulwich, 94
Free Methodist chapel, Bellenden Road, 62, 93-5, 96, 98, 118

Gauntlett, Edwin, printer's manager and churchwarden, 36, 37, 62-3, 96, 101 n1, 109
Gauntlett, Mrs, 96
The Glebe, Grove Hill, Camberwell, 56-8
   see also Grove Hill
Grove Hill, Camberwell, 2, 3, 17, 61, 118
Grove Hill Road, Denmark Park, 5, 6, 8, 9, 13-15, 17, 25, 27
Grove Park, Camberwell, 3, 7, 61-2, 66 n5
Grove Vale, East Dulwich, 18, 80, 101 n8
   Estate, 17, 101 n8
   Imperial Hall, 110
Guy's Hospital, 103

Hanover Congregational chapel, Peckham, 95, 119 n9
Harnden, Joseph, of Copleston Road, 64

Haslam, John, vicar of St Saviour's, 38, 39, 43-6, 48-51, 57, 58, 60, 70, 72, 74, 80, 89-90, 98, 100, 103, 114
Haslam, Mrs, 64-5
Hastie, J Hepburn, of Champion Park, Camberwell, 61
Heard family, of Copleston Road, 64
Henderson, James, proprietor of the *South London Press*, 109, 119 n1
Holy Trinity, New Beckenham, 23, 41 n16
Horniman, Frederick, tea merchant, 32 n4
hospitals, 103
housing, 3, 5-9, 14, 29
Hughes, William Barnsley, architect, 26, 31

Ivanhoe Road, Denmark Park, 5-7, 9, 15, 62
   Hotel, 7, 110

Johnston, Thomas, medical practitioner and churchwarden, 62
Jones, E Herbert, curate of St Saviour's, 39
Jones, Edwin, department store proprietor, 109
Jones and Higgins, Peckham department store, 109, 110

Kelly, Francis F, vicar of St Giles's, 91
King, Edward, bishop of Lincoln, 37, 102
Kleinwort, Alexander, of The Glebe, Grove Hill, banker, 58

labourers, *see* working class
Lava Skating Rink, Denmark Hill, 57-8
Lawrence, Sir JC, MP for Lambeth, 94
Lewis, AH, of Copleston Road, 73
Lightfoot, John, of Copleston Road, 63, 66 n8
lodgers, 14, 15
London
   bishop of, xii
   County Council, 98, 109
   population of, xi-xii, 24
   see also School Board for London; South London
lower middle class, 5, 12-14, 18, 63, 95, 99, 100, 110, 111, 116-17
Lutheran chapel, Denmark Hill, 58
Lyndhurst Road (later Way), Peckham, 83

McDermott, Bryen, of Peckham Rye, cheesemonger and landowner, 2
Malfort Road, Denmark Park, 5, 9
Maxted Road, Peckham, 27-9, 90

INDEX

middle class, 13, 60, 61, 72, 95, 100, 109, 116
  see also lower middle class

New Choumert Road, *see* Choumert Road
Nunhead, xiv
  see also St Silas's

Oglander Road, East Dulwich, 27-9, 78, 80, 90
  Tavern, 110
Ottley, RL, canon of Christ Church, Oxford, 89
owner-occupation, 3, 7, 17

parishes
  creation of, xii-xiii
  size of, xi
  see also boundaries, parish
parochial consciousness, 79-84, 85 n3, 85 n6 and n7, 105, 117
Peckham, xiv, 16, 93, 95, 103, 104, 109
  St Mary's College, 100
  Tonic Sol-fa Choir, 95
  see also Hanover Congregational chapel; Peckham Rye
Peckham Rye, 2
  Common, 111
  Estate, 6-9, 11-18, 27, 60, 80, 93, 99, 108, 109
  Park, 111
  Station, 6, 83
Peek, Francis, tea merchant and philanthropist, 22-31, 34, 38, 46, 49, 98, 100
Peek, Sir Henry, 1st Bt, 22, 24-5
politics, party, 94, 95, 99, 108-11
population, local, xiii-xiv, 11, 15, 17, 56, 57
  see also London

railways, 17, 108, 117, 119 n8
  London and Sutton line (L, B and SCR), 2, 5, 6
  South London line (L, B and SCR), 7
rateable values, 5, 9
rents, house, xiv, 16, 17
ritualism, 23, 36-7, 63
Rochester
  bishop of, *see* Talbot, Edward; Thorold, Anthony
  diocese of, xiii, 38, 90, 108
Rotherhithe, 24, 32 n9
Rumble family, of Choumert Road, church activists, 63-4
Rye Lane, Peckham, 110
  see also Jones and Higgins

St Agnes's, Kennington Park, 85 n6
St Barnabas's, Dulwich, 31
St Bartholomew's, Sydenham, 23
St Clement's, East Dulwich, 30, 41 n12, 80, 92 n6
St George's, Camberwell, 106
St Giles's, Camberwell, 27, 61, 69, 83-4, 87, 88, 90-1
St James's, Hatcham, 85 n6
St John the Evangelist, Goose Green, East Dulwich, xiii, xiv, 11, 24-5, 27-9, 30, 34, 69, 78, 83, 84, 87, 88, 90, 99, 101 n6, 106, 113
St John's, Penge, 24
St Luke's, Deptford, 106
St Mark's, Walworth, xvi n2
St Mary's, Haggerston, 106
St Michael and All Angels, Croydon, xii
St Paul's, Lorrimore Square, Walworth, 43, 80, 85 n6
St Peter's, Dulwich Common, 25, 113
St Saviour's, Champion Hill, *see* St Saviour's, Denmark Park
St Saviour's, Denmark Park
  baptisms, 35, 60-1, 68, 69, 81-4, 86-8
  bazaars, 57-8, 59 n9, 64, 66 n14
  bible classes, 47, 64, 72
  charitable activities, 54, 72-3, 79, 80, 103-6
  choir, *see* music
  church, 25-7, 43-4
  Church House (50 Copleston Road), 49-50, 51, 55, 57, 58, 106, 119 n9
  Church Lodge (72 Avondale Road), 49, 75
  churchwardens, 36, 61-3, 79
  Church Workers' Society, 48, 71, 73, 74
  clergy, *see* curates; vicars
  communicants, 36, 37, 48, 60, 67
  Confirmations, 47
  cricket club, 39, 49, 50, 73, 74
  curates, 30, 38, 39-40, 49, 54, 56; *and see* Carolin, J Sinclair; Jones, E Herbert; Smith, Alan Gordon; Sturt, Horace; Wilkin, WH
  deaf and dumb services, 91
  Easter offertory, 30, 56, 111
  finances and fund-raising, 54-8
  Guild of the Love of Jesus, 48
  Guild of St Saviour's, 48, 73-4, 90
  harvest festivals, 45, 105
  Hospital Sunday, 45, 56, 103
  incumbents, *see* vicars
  Institute (93 Choumert Road), 46, 49, 72, 74, 119 n9
  lay readers, 46, 47
  living, 29-30

mission room, *see* Institute
mission services, 46, 72
Mothers' Meeting, 73, 80, 91
music, 34, 35, 36, 44, 54
organs, organists, *see* music
parish boundaries, 27-9, 61, 117
parish magazine, 46, 47, 50, 79-80
patronage, 27
pew rents, *see* seat rents
seat rents, 30, 54-6, 72
services, 34, 37, 38, 44-6, 54, 70-1, 116
social activities, 36, 49-50, 70, 73-5; *and see* cricket club; tennis club
Sunday school, 36, 40, 47, 48, 51, 55, 64, 72, 100, 103, 105, 112 n9
tennis club, 74-5
vestry, 36, 50-1, 79
Vicarage, 9, 25, 27, 65, 105, 118
vicars, *see* Daukes, FW; Haslam, John; Stephenson, JJ; Swithinbank, HS
visitors, lady, 39, 47-8, 64, 79, 103, 105
St Saviour's, Southwark, later Southwark Cathedral, 90, 91
St Silas's, Nunhead, 31
St Thomas's Hospital, 103
School Board for London, 23, 98, 109
  see also Bellenden Road Board School
Second World War, 118
service, domestic, 8, 13-14, 15-16, 42 n23, 72
shopkeepers, 13, 95
Smith, Alan Gordon, curate of St Saviour's, 39, 74, 104
South London
  Church in, 90-1
  dissent in, 93
  expansion of, xiii-xiv
  social composition of, xiv, 17
  social life in, 108-11
South London Press, xiii, 5, 36, 63, 109, 110, 113
  see also Henderson, James
Southwark, xii
  diocese of, 90
  Evelina Hospital, 103
Spurgeon, Charles Haddon, Baptist minister, 37

Stephenson, John Joseph, vicar of St Saviour's, 24, 34-5, 43-6, 50, 51, 56, 70, 71-2, 80, 114
Strickland, WJ, vicar of St John's, 90
Sturt, Horace, curate of St Saviour's, 39
Swithinbank, Herbert Spencer, vicar of St Saviour's, 35-8, 39, 43, 45-9, 51, 62, 70, 73, 74, 80, 83, 89, 96, 98, 99, 101 n4, 103, 105, 111, 114
Swithinbank, Mrs, 99

Talbot, Edward, bishop of Rochester, 38, 51, 89, 91
Talfourd Road, Peckham, 5
Ten Churches Fund, 30
Terry, Edward, of Bellenden Road, builder, 26, 29, 109
Thorold, Anthony, bishop of Rochester, xiv, xvi n11, 24, 27, 30, 34, 35, 43
transport, 6, 7, 17-18, 80, 110
  see also railways
Tunbridge Wells, Kent, 22, 26

Unitarian chapel, Avondale Road, 93-4, 101 n1

Victoria Tavern, Victoria (later Bellenden) Road, 27, 76 n14, 109

Walworth, xii
  see also St Mark's; St Paul's, Lorrimore Square
Warburton, Thomas, vicar of St John's, 24-5, 27, 99
West Dulwich, 23
Westrup family, of Copleston Road, church activists, 63-4
  Sir Jack, 66 n12
Wilkin, WH, curate of St Saviour's, 39
Winch, William, tea merchant, 27
Winchester, diocese of, xiii, 108
women, role of, 63, 64-5, 73, 75, 105, 110
Wood, Miss Elizabeth, of The Glebe, Grove Hill, 56-7, 61, 66 n4
Wood, William, of The Glebe, Grove Hill, merchant, 56, 61
working class, 13

Yarrow Home, Broadstairs, 104, 107 n6